W0018212

SAGE was founded in 1965 by Sara Miller McCune to support the dissemination of usable knowledge by publishing innovative and high-quality research and teaching content. Today, we publish more than 850 journals, including those of more than 300 learned societies, more than 800 new books per year, and a growing range of library products including archives, data, case studies, reports, conference highlights, and video. SAGE remains majority-owned by our founder, and after Sara's lifetime will become owned by a charitable trust that secures our continued independence.

Los Angeles | London | New Delhi | Singapore | Washington DC

Human
Drama Inc.

Bulk Sales

SAGE India offers special discounts
for purchase of books in bulk.
We also make available special imprints
and excerpts from our books on demand.

For orders and enquiries, write to us at

Marketing Department
SAGE Publications India Pvt Ltd
B1/I-1, Mohan Cooperative Industrial Area
Mathura Road, Post Bag 7
New Delhi 110044, India

E-mail us at **marketing@sagepub.in**

Get to know more about SAGE

Be invited to SAGE events, get on our mailing list.
Write today to **marketing@sagepub.in**

This book is also available as an e-book.

Human
Drama Inc.

Emotional Intelligence
in the Workplace

Neeta Mohla

www.sagepublications.com

Los Angeles • London • New Delhi • Singapore • Washington DC

First published in 2015 by

SAGE Response
B1/I-1 Mohan Cooperative Industrial Area
Mathura Road, New Delhi 110 044, India

SAGE Publications Inc
2455 Teller Road
Thousand Oaks, California 91320, USA

SAGE Publications Ltd
1 Oliver's Yard, 55 City Road
London EC1Y 1SP, United Kingdom

SAGE Publications Asia-Pacific Pte Ltd
3 Church Street
#10-04 Samsung Hub
Singapore 049483

Published by Vivek Mehra for SAGE Publications India Pvt Ltd, typeset in 11/13 Century Book by Zaza Eunice, Hosur, India and printed at Sai Print-o-pack, New Delhi.

Library of Congress Cataloging-in-Publication Data

Mohla, Neeta.
  Human drama Inc. : emotional intelligence in the workplace / Neeta Mohla.
      pages cm
  1. Emotional intelligence. 2. Social interaction. 3. Self-presentation. 4. Success. I. Title.
  BF576.M64   158.7—dc23   2015   2015021223

ISBN: 978-93-515-0290-6 (PB)

The SAGE Team: Sachin Sharma, Sandhya Gola, Nand Kumar Jha and Vinitha Nair

Contents

Foreword

Human Drama Inc. may appear to be a book that highlights only the play of emotions in the work situations. In reality, it is a far more profound and insightful piece of writing on human dynamics not only in the workplace but also in the life of each one of us in the contemporary organisations and society. It reminds us of the famous couplet by Alexander Pope: 'Know then thyself, presume not God to scan. The proper study of Mankind is Man.'

The book aims at helping managers and leaders to understand, gain insights and apply the concepts related to *emotional intelligence* in the typical human dilemmas that we encounter at workplace, family life and personal growth in the rapidly changing modern society and organisations in India. It does so in a very unconventional manner, basing its narrative on real-life stories of persons whose existential dilemmas and experiences become the source material for analysis and understanding of the complexities of human behaviour and emotions, and how to deal with them for personal development, interpersonal skills and team effectiveness.

As we all know, organisations work on the tacit assumption that human behaviour is basically rational and logical, and that domain knowledge and expertise are the keys to making individuals in organisations efficient, effective, innovative and productive. The non-logical, emotional aspects of behaviour are generally considered *irrational* and *immature*. Thus, intelligence quotient (IQ), technical knowledge and expertise get priority in selection and promotion, without taking into account the skill set required for the supervisory and managerial roles, as individuals advance in their career. The crisis that many technically bright persons face when promoted as team leaders and managers is quite common and well known. It is assumed that a technically competent person will automatically acquire human and conceptual skills to deal with intrapersonal, interpersonal, teamworking and other organisational effectiveness issues. Paradoxically, the reality is quite different, as all successful leaders and managers know.

In the words of Daniel Goleman, the leading thinker, researcher and writer on emotional intelligence, as quoted in the book:[1]

If your emotional abilities aren't in hand, if you don't have self-awareness, if you are not able to manage your distressing emotions, if you can't have empathy and have effective relationships, then no matter how smart you are, you are not going to get very far.

The book is anchored in the context of Indian culture. To illustrate the importance of the various concepts related to emotional intelligence, it borrows wisdom from the concept of 'navras' from *Natya Shastra*. The author draws upon her rich training and consulting experience in addition to the findings of some well-known researches to analyse the nuances of culture in the Indian organisations.

The author has taken up specific elements of emotional intelligence and helps the readers to gain insights by real-life stories of persons whose experiences are vividly described, and then insights are highlighted. Perceptive analysis of human dynamics underlying the story is presented as 'behind-the-scenes' narrative. The practical exercises are given as 'toolbox' for introspection, analysis and application of concepts for developing intrapersonal, interpersonal and team-related human skills.

---

[1] Daniel Goleman, 1995, cited in: John O. Dozier, 2010, *The Weeping, The Window, The Way*, p. 130.

After covering all the key elements of emotional intelligence within the self, and then dealing with its social dimensions, the book focuses on application of emotional intelligence in critical organisational issues such as change, conflict, customer service, productivity, performance management and inspirational leadership.

One para of the book that succinctly encapsulates the wisdom of relating emotional intelligence to leadership is as follows:

The leadership challenge of focusing on the right issues, while developing people to enable them to take on more responsibilities and achieve higher results efficiently, continues to exist. Mature leaders, who are not fraught with the fear of losing their jobs in an extremely competitive environment, are seen to develop their teams. Courageous and empathic leaders, who speak their mind while exploring the feelings and views of their subordinates effectively, develop their people. Optimistic leaders, who see things objectively, yet push the bar for their teams believing in their capabilities, develop their people. But most of all, leaders who enjoy people and the process of giving of themselves to see others grow, develop others. Such leaders have to be strong in emotional intelligence, as a number of components such as objectivity, self-expression, achievement drive, optimism, empathy and interpersonal skills are required to be a truly successful leader.

In a limited space of about 190 pages, the book covers a wide range of human dilemmas in the personal, family and work life of persons working in contemporary organisations. In fact, it transcends the boundaries between the personal, family and work life, which is a more realistic and holistic presentation of life's dilemmas, than the *silo* perspective that most books on management and behavioural theory and practice seem to follow.

The format and style of presentation make it a highly readable and absorbing book that the readers find easy to relate to their own situations, and find answers for dealing with complex human dynamics in their lives.

In my opinion, this book is very helpful for personal growth and interpersonal effectiveness, especially for the persons already in or aspiring to rise in managerial and leadership roles. I will particularly recommend it to the Masters in Business Administration (MBA) and Postgraduate Diploma in Management (PGDM) students, most of who come from engineering background, which sometimes limits the development of critical human skills such as self-awareness and empathy that are essential for their success in managerial career. Similarly, I would recommend the book as a *must-read* supportive material for behavioural training, personal development and counselling/coaching process in organisations.

Professor Abad Ahmad
Former Pro-Vice Chancellor and Dean,
Faculty of Management Studies,
University of Delhi

Acknowledgements

When you are not an author, when you are someone who believes that great thoughts and ideas come when there is participation from like and unlike minds, it is truly important to acknowledge and thank each and everyone who made this book possible.

My first thanks goes to TMI and Claus Møller. I learnt my lessons on emotional intelligence; thanks to this great organisation and its creator.

My colleague Ankita Sinha has been the backbone in our dream project of writing this book. At every instance, it was her support, research and tireless doggedness that pushed the book through. Without her commitment to help with the text, the research and the immense follow-up, including with me, I do not believe the book would have been possible.

Several colleagues from work contributed to the stories, which they had gathered as part of their consulting experience in the area of emotional intelligence. To Suman, Saumya, Alka, Ashuma, Anupama and Puja—a special thanks. You brought in variety and perspectives, and this made it so much more interesting.

To many of my supporters and clients who always find a moment to give us their counsel and who helped in reviewing the manuscripts despite so many preoccupations, I am highly indebted. Thank you, Professor Abad, Khurshid Bandyopadhyay, Dr Sharada Ganesh, Savita Kriplani and Carmistha Mitra.

A special mention must be made to the team at Grammar Gurus—Pallavi and Piya. Their tips on building the audience connect were very crucial, especially for a first-timer like me.

My family, also my world—first, my true critic, my unlike mind, my husband, Deepak. Phew! Thanks for *pushing the bar*—it works perfectly with my need for approval. On a more serious note, your ideas and brilliant thinking always inspire. I would never have got to this without you.

My four children (sons and daughters-in-law), who have always been a big support.

Mayura and Dave—our family authors! Your encouragement and support came at the right time. Thank you.

And finally, my father—he was my mentor. His belief, incredible encouragement and love made me *want* to write. I know he would be proud wherever he is.

Introduction to Emotional Intelligence

CREATING VALUE FOR ORGANISATIONS: ROLE OF HUMAN CAPITAL

Traditionally, capital in organisations comprised physical assets such as land, plant and machinery, and financial assets such as inventory and cash. The balance sheets of companies hence represented these assets as the key capital of the organisation. These assets were considered investments for the future.

People, however, were never considered assets in the true sense of the word in the accounting system, even though every manager touted the much popular line: 'People are our most valuable assets.' People-related expenses such as salaries and development costs have always been shown as costs in the profit and loss statements of accounts.

This belief has changed a lot in the last decade. Empirical data and research have shown that intangible assets, *patents, brands, company processes, customer loyalty* and *human capital*, account for a substantial part of the value of organisations, especially in the modern knowledge economy. For instance, in the early 2000s, the value of U.S. intangible assets (almost US$ 3.4 trillion) accounted for more than 75 per cent of U.S. output growth.

Besides, there is a qualitative link between intangible assets and firm performance.[1] The real value for an organisation comes not only from a strong strategy but also from its reputation, the loyalty of its customers, the ability to

---

[1] A. Arrighetti, F. Landin and A. Lasagni, 2014, 'Intangible assets and firm heterogeneity: Evidence from Italy', *Research Policy*, 43(1), 202–213.

innovate and create constant value for its customers and the positive relationships built by its people.

The need and importance of human capital has been felt by organisations significantly in the last 10 years. This includes the value of educational qualifications, skills, strengths and the ability to leverage people's capability, commitment and experience. It is also about the way in which employees work together and about the relationships they have both inside and outside the organisation. Most organisations today are aware that besides paying good salaries, the enhancement of human capital is all about ensuring challenging assignments, stretch goals, flexible structures, bonuses and equity and effective leadership. In fact, it is human capital that creates the biggest value for the organisation by driving all other elements of intangible assets/ intellectual capital such as brand capital, customer capital, knowledge capital and relationship capital. As human capital pushes the value of organisations by building its intellectual capital, leadership behaviour is the single largest determinant on which human capital is dependant.

Research estimates that while companies could easily add 10–20 per cent to their operating income by better utilising human capital, only a small number reach even the 0.5 per cent mark. Suffice to say, companies are leaving a wealth of value in their intellectual assets unrealised.

If human capital is central to creating value, emotional intelligence represents the key to unlock this potential.

EMOTIONAL INTELLIGENCE

The term *emotional intelligence* consists of two basic elements: *emotion* and *intelligence*. Each of these elements has an interesting history.

The word 'emotion' does not have one clear definition. The derivation of the word according to the Webster

Dictionary is as follows: from Latin, *exmovere* (to move out) and *emovere* (to move away), and from French, *emouvoir* (to start out, to incite, to stir up) and *mouvoir* (to move).

Emotions have been dealt with by philosophers since ancient times. In the second part of the 20th century, the study of emotions became part of the new science of psychology.

Up until around 1960, psychology primarily dealt with mental abilities, intelligence testing, personality assessment and the treatment of people with emotional problems.

Emotional Intelligence refers to the capacity for recognising our own feelings and that of others, for motivating ourselves, and for managing emotions well in ourselves and in our relationships.

— D. Goleman

From 1960 onwards, psychology has been employed more and more in corporate life to build better teams and improve interpersonal relationships inspired by contributions from people such as Eric Berne (*Games People Play*) and Andrew Mayo (*The Human Side of the Enterprise*).[2]

The popular psychological topics that have been introduced into the business world have been Gestalt therapy, transactional analysis, neurolinguistic programming (NLP), active listening, stress management, positive thinking, team building and, most recently, emotional intelligence.

---

[2] Adapted from TMI's Heart Work by, Claus Møller; Eric Berne, *Games People Play*, 1973, New York: Ballantine Books; Andrew Mayo, 2001, *The Human Value of the Enterprise*, London: Nicholas Brealey.

The study of human intelligence can be traced back to the end of the 19th century when the first intelligence tests were being developed. By the beginning of the 20th century, the first IQ tests began to be used, and millions of people have been tested with such measures since then.

As a strong reaction against the IQ approach, Gardner introduced his seven intelligence concepts, including intrapersonal and interpersonal intelligence, in 1983.

In the early 1980s, Bar-On began to develop the concept of emotional intelligence, and in the 1990s, a number of other emotional intelligence definitions and concepts were introduced by people such as Sternberg, Goleman, Salovey and Mayer.

Soon, significant research in organisational behaviour revealed that in the top ranks of many multinationals were people who were smart in ways that had nothing to do with IQ scores; by the end of the 20th century, feelings, emotions and social skills that had hitherto been devalued by science began to gain prominence.

Emotional intelligence is not the opposite of IQ; rather, it complements IQ. Intellect dictates our educational choices and career paths, but as you climb up the ladder, social and emotional abilities gain prominence. Personal qualities such as empathy, adaptability, persuasiveness, openness to change and willingness to diversify are the factors that help to actualise individual potential.

DEFINING EMOTIONAL INTELLIGENCE

The framework and definitions used in this book draw from TMI's framework of emotional intelligence, on which I was trained. In this concept, emotional intelligence consists of two broad capacities—interpersonal and intrapersonal, which are further divided into 15 components, as pictured in the following table:

TMI's Personal Emotional Intelligence (EI) Concept

5 EI areas and 15 EI components

Self-awareness (knowing one's emotions)

Self-appraisal
Knowing one's inner resources, abilities and limitations.

Emotional self-awareness
Recognising and understanding one's emotions

Objectivity
Validating one's feelings and thoughts.

Self-expression
Expressing feelings, beliefs and thoughts in a non-destructive way.

Self-management (managing one's emotions)

Stress management
Actively coping with adverse events and stressful situations.

Impulse control
Controlling disruptive emotions and impulses.

Self-reliance
Being independent in one's thinking and behaviour

Adaptability
Being flexible and willing to change

Problem-solving
Generating and implementing potentially effective solutions to daily problems

Self-motivation (motivating oneself)

Optimism
Expecting the best outcome, even in the face of adversity

Achievement drive
Striving to realise one's potential

Contentment
Having a positive approach to life and enjoying oneself

Intrapersonal capacity

(Continued)

(*Continued*)

5 EI areas and 15 EI components	
Interpersonal capacity	**Social awareness** (recognising emotions in others)
	Empathy Recognising, understanding and appreciating others' feelings, needs and concerns.
	Social skills (managing relationship)
	Interpersonal relations Establishing and maintaining relationships.
	Group orientation Feeling part of a group and being a co-operative and contributing member.

Source: TMI's Heart Work by Claus Møller.

EMOTIONAL INTELLIGENCE IN THE INDIAN CONTEXT

In India, the high diversity in culture, language, education system and income adds a unique layer of complexity to the work environment.

Since the 1960s, scholars have been interested in the relationship between culture and various emotional phenomena. Cultures vary on a number of fundamental values, attitudes and assumptions, including:

1. Display and feeling rules
2. Values attached to events and their importance
3. Experiences and attitudes with which one evaluates and handles emotions
4. Appraisal of events
5. Behaviour generation[3]

---

[3] C.E. Izard, 1980, 'Cross-cultural Perspectives on Emotion and Emotion Communication'. In H. Triandis and W. Lonner (Eds), *Handbook of Cross-cultural Psychology*, pp. 23–45. Boston: Allyn & Bacon.

While India is not mentioned explicitly in Edward Hall's research on high- and low-context cultures, it is believed that India can be categorised as a high-context culture. In such cultures, communication style is influenced by the closeness of human relationships, well-structured social hierarchy and strong behavioural norms.[4]

In a high-context culture, meaning is often embedded deep in the information, so not everything is explicitly stated in writing or when spoken. The listener is expected to be able to read *between the lines*, to understand the unsaid, thanks to his or her background knowledge. In such a culture, people tend to rely on their history, their status, their relationships and a range of other information, including religion, to assign meaning to an event.

A few aspects of emotional intelligence draw from India's ancient yogic traditions; for example, the real meaning of yoga is the process of self-realisation, leading to a super-personal sense of self—that is, a heightened level of consciousness. At times, this self-awareness naturally gives rise to genuine empathy, that is, seeing the self in others.

A major dimension of culture appears to be individualistic versus collectivist. India is a moderately collectivist culture (scoring 48 on the individualism scale), suggesting the presence of both collectivist and individualistic characteristics in India. This indicates that in India people think of themselves as part of interdependent groups, giving higher priority to the needs of their in-group than to their personal goals. They are also likely to use in-group norms to shape their behaviour, rather than personal attitudes. The mindset in India points towards a clear family orientation; although individual members have a great flexibility in adapting to the collective norms, they are often passive in proposing new ideas.

---

[4] D. Kim, Y. Pan and H.S. Park, 1998. 'High- versus low-context culture: A comparison of Chinese, Korean and American cultures', *Psychology & Marketing*, 15(6), 507–521.

Such cultural dimensions have an effect on cognitive, affective and motivational processes. For instance, the overt expression of emotions is restrained in interdependent cultures, and a sense of achievement includes familial and social concerns such as fulfilling duties and helping others. In later work on culture, Hofstede included another dimension of *long-term orientation* in his research on collectivist cultures and found that India scored 61 on this cultural value, signifying the importance of perseverance and thrift in Indian society. Indian culture is highly complex and pluralistic, containing seemingly inconsistent and contradictory orientations. Indians, for example, are observed to be polite, non-assertive, emotional and tolerant in some of their orientations. These characteristics, however, are juxtaposed with a strong need for material influence, power and control and status in society.

In addition to national cultures, organisational and professional cultures also have an influence on the way emotions are perceived, interpreted and acted upon.[5]

THE INDIAN WORKPLACE

In a survey of Indian employees working for foreign companies, Gabeler[6] found that most respondents felt that a boss should be strict and must maintain discipline by monitoring and reviewing the work activities of the subordinates. It is the boss who decides and looks for solutions. He is the one

---

[5] F. Shipper, J. Kincaid, M.D. Rotondo and C.R. Hoffman IV, 2003, 'A Cross-cultural exploratory study of the linkage between emotional intelligence and managerial effectiveness', *The International Journal of Organizational Analysis*, 11(3), 171–191.

[6] J. Gabeler, 1996, *Intercultural Co-operation between Germans and Indians*, Unpublished study for Deutsche Gesellschaft für Technische Zusammenarbeit.

who should set an example by showing dedication to the work and to his subordinates.

In India, there is a general dependence on those who hold power, and Indians need plenty of communication and directions from the top for the completion of their work. The process of execution is also tightly monitored through frequent follow-ups by the supervisor. Thus, communication tends to be more top-downwards than bottom-upwards.

Furthermore, the subordinates' basic willingness to have a close relationship with their superiors and to identify with them is extremely high too. This closeness to one's supervisor is an implicit status symbol for the subordinate, indicating that they are part of the 'in-group'.

In the Indian context, an initial focus on building good relationships creates a good foundation for the ultimate goal of task orientation. It has been pointed out that this ideal dual leadership style (often termed 'nurturant–task leadership style') has greater chances of success in India because Indians have a prominent relational need; a superior's personal interest in his subordinates' life may have a magnetic touch, and it galvanises them into action. A motivated subordinate employee would go to any extent to meet their superior's expectations, feel secure and trusted, and have a sense of belonging to the organisation.

However, there are variations within Indian culture as well. Software companies in South India operate primarily on the Western egalitarian pattern and may not fit into the Indian mode. On the other hand, small-scale businesses (e.g., in retail trade) are organised very much like a family, where the eldest member of the family runs and leads the business within a system of authority, all members have set roles, and conforming to rules is beneficial to all. The situation in medium-sized (or semi-professional) organisations is a hybrid of the traditional stereotype and a bid to catch up with the new ways of doing things (e.g., hiring of MBA graduates). The work culture at large Indian multinational corporations

(MNCs) may be considered professional and, in many ways, more Western than Indian.

To summarise, the acceptance of organisational hierarchy, readiness to accept change (or acceptance of risk/unknown outcomes), participation and identification in group activity (or collectivism) and perseverance at work broadly describe the four major values in Indian business world and work culture.

INSIGHTS FROM OUR WORK ON EMOTIONAL INTELLIGENCE

Our work with different organisations across India over the last two decades has given us an in-depth understanding of the role of emotional intelligence in Indian workplace culture. Here are a few of our key observations:

1. The expression of emotions at the workplace is not a *taboo*. Emotions are expressed freely by leaders, both in politics and in business.
2. In most organisations, there is a predominant dependence on the 'leader' of the group. This is especially true of family businesses where the patriarchal system is very visible at the workplace—people in the system look for the leader and can seldom challenge his views directly. In such systems, emotionally intelligent people learn to pick up cues from the leader and manoeuvre their way *through* the system rather than directly confronting it. Trust with the boss is a big asset and plays a key role in being successful—often, this may be based on factors other than competence. The workplace embodies the personal values of the leader.

    Dissent in this type of system is possible, but mostly leads to breakaways as opposed to creating new solutions within the existing structure. This is also validated by research.[7] In high-power distance cultures such as India, subordinates expect autocratic leadership, hesitate to disagree with their superiors, tolerate superiors' questionable practices and tend to obey superiors' unethical instructions. In contrast, low-power distance cultures (e.g., Australia, Canada) foster a more interdependent and egalitarian relationship between superiors and subordinates.

3. Loyalty based on strong relationships forms the basis of building businesses. It is also the main driving factor for people extending themselves and going the extra mile at work, as opposed to things such as professional ethics or professional goals. Essentially, Indian organisations tend to be people and relationship oriented, with lesser focus on processes. With the advent of multinational organisations, things are slowly starting to change. By and large, however, loyalty remains a cornerstone of Indian corporate culture.

4. On the one hand, family values and traditions typically play a vital role in dealing with situations in India; on the other hand, 'rules and regulations' are not seen as integral at the workplace. There is a fairly low acceptance of rules in Indian companies. This sporadically leads to the development of entrepreneurial spirit, but it also causes low workplace efficiency and productivity in general.

Overall, there appears to be an understanding of emotional intelligence concept in the Indian context as well as a visible demonstration of the same in society and leadership. This makes it very possible to harness the potential of emotional intelligence in the growth story of the nation.

---

[7] A. Ilangovan, W.A. Scroggins and E.J. Rozeh, 2007, 'Managerial perspectives on emotional intelligence differences between India and the United States: The development of research propositions, *International Journal of Management*, 24(3), 541–548.

Know More: Emotional Experience in the Indian Context

In the Indian context, every event or work of art is denoted by a dominant emotional theme called *rasa* (literally 'juice' or 'essence'), which is the primary feeling that is evoked in the person who views, reads or hears such a work. 'Navras' is the aesthetic experience (not the emotional experience itself) of the nine basic emotions or tastes (rasas), namely, sensitive (perception of love, shringar), comic (*hasya*), heroic (*veer*), furious (*raudra*), apprehensive (*vibhatsa*), compassionate (*karuna*), horrific (*bhayanak*), marvellous (*adbhut*) and calm (*shaant*).

The nine rasas are the essential aspects or energies that define a set of emotions and moods that thus belong to the same family or Rasa. While the nine Rasas themselves are clearly defined energies affecting body and mind, the resulting emotions (*bhavas*) manifest in many varieties and their understanding is affected by personal and cultural backgrounds. Knowing the nine rasas helps us to understand why a certain mood comes and stays even though its original cause may be long gone and how to use that knowledge in achieving more emotional control.

Rasa Sadhana is an ancient tantric tradition of emotional fasting. When doing *sadhana* of anger, for example, whenever something irritating occurs, just remembering our promise not to give in to anger will create a distance between us and the angry feeling. Through such regular exercises, it is believed that we can learn to master our nine rasas, which will soon start to happen quite effortlessly.

ACT 1   Knowing the Script

Do You Understand Your Character and Role?

Self-awareness

'Take control of the little choices you have every day as these will shape the big decisions in your life.'

INTRODUCTION TO SELF-AWARENESS

Many times, we feel as though we have no choice in how our lives play out. What we do not realise is that our life is being shaped every day in every way by the small decisions we make—how we respond to the people in our lives, to a changing circumstance, to a new opportunity, to feedback, to challenges, to expectations, to our cultural context. While these things may seem beyond our control, our reactions and actions in relation to these circumstances are fully in our grasp—what it means is that *if* we have the self-awareness to deal with these inputs in a way that shape a positive destiny.

Self-awareness is the first and perhaps most important principle amongst the factors that make up emotional intelligence. Quite simply, self-awareness is the ability to know one's emotions. The four qualities that constitute self-awareness are:

- *Self-appraisal*: Knowing ones inner resources, abilities and limitations.
- *Emotional self-awareness*: Recognising and understanding one's emotions.
- *Objectivity:* Validating one's feelings and thoughts.
- *Self-expression:* Expressing feelings, beliefs and thoughts in a non-destructive way.

In this section, you will find a series of stories that illustrate these four components. At various points in the stories, you will be given an insight into how individuals use the power of self-awareness to navigate and create the life that they want and deserve. Some of the stories will be followed by an exercise for you to complete. You will also be given tools with which you can use these self-awareness concepts tangibly in your daily life.

SCENE 1

Looking into the Mirror

Self-appraisal

'The one self-knowledge worth having is to know one's own mind.'

~ F. H. Bradley

KAMAL'S STORY: SETTING THE SCENE FOR SUCCESS

Kamal looked at his self-appraisal scores with delight. Nine out of ten was good by all accounts. As the consultant explained what this meant—*awareness of his strengths and weaknesses, accepting himself for who he is, feeling fulfilled and inviting feedback*—Kamal could not agree more. Today, he was at the place he had most wanted to be. What could be more fulfilling?

Born into a middle-class family where a government job had been the family norm for generations, Kamal had always dreamt of being a film-maker. He passionately wanted to create the kind of cinema that would hugely impact people—taking up social issues and creating a change. All along, he had opted for activities that aligned with his strengths and his goals. While almost his whole class had opted for commerce for the Class X exam, Kamal was sure that fine arts and psychology were what he wanted to take. Thankfully, the school offered these courses.

> To create the life and career that you want, you must have the self-awareness to know what truly drives and fulfils you. Only then will you gain the clarity and focus needed to pursue your dreams and goals.

Kamal's family as always shared their viewpoint with him, but seeing his steely determination, they went along with his choices. The only condition that they had was that Kamal should also take up mathematics and history; they believed that should Kamal change his mind upon leaving school, this would help him in his civil services exams.

Kamal was a calm and clear-headed person with a great knack for communication, specially written communication. He had great ideas and strong views about occurrences around him, combined with a somewhat caustic sense of humour. Hard work, focus and concentration came easily to him, and though he was not the most flamboyant or affable person in his batch, he had a good circle of friends who respected his views. His attachment to his family was apparent—he saw them as a source of encouragement and appreciation. And though strangers often mistook his reserve and his focus on his goals as arrogance, his acquaintances and friends found Kamal steady and dependable.

> Pay special note to how Kamal deals with compromise in his life—balancing his family's expectations with his own.

His school results were not surprising. Kamal had always topped his class, and the final results once again confirmed this. Kamal felt the reason he did so well was that he knew exactly what he wanted. He was aware of his strengths and his weaknesses, and knowing this helped him use his strengths in most situations. He realised that working around strengths was always easier and more effective as he could demonstrate excellence easily; he also had no trouble seeking help in areas where he was weak. While he worked on his weaknesses, he worked equally hard at his strengths because he knew that was what would give him the edge. This also meant that his self-esteem was always high, and negative energies were kept at a low.

> Knowing your strengths and seeking feedback on areas of improvement are powerful allies in achieving your goals.

Kamal's results ensured that he got into the prestigious St Xavier's College without a problem. His friends and family were delighted. His family secretly hoped that this might make Kamal more favourably inclined towards the Indian Administrative Service (IAS) or Indian Foreign Service (IFS). Kamal enrolled for sociology honours, a subject close to his heart, but also decided to apply for a coveted scholarship at Cambridge (UK), which would enable him to opt for subjects such as film-making and film critiquing—something that would bring him closer to realising his dream.

At the end of his first year at college, Kamal received the news that he had won the scholarship for a social sciences course at King's College (University of Cambridge). Four years and many accolades later, Harrison Consulting Group decided to visit the campus to recruit the brightest students. As per their strategy, the organisation had decided to expand its search to identify analysts from a number of different fields (not just from the usual business schools) to bring diversity into the organisation. Kamal, of course, was selected.

The family was thrilled that Kamal had made the move to get into consulting, which seemed to be a more *acceptable* career choice. However, the real reason Kamal had joined—which he had stated in his interview—was the opportunity to work in consulting projects with different governments to find solutions to social issues that countries face.

Very soon, Kamal was taking a flight to Baghdad to work closely with victims of war and to help create social policies that would have a big impact on the people of that country.

Kamal loved his job—not for the money it gave him, but for the ability to see social issues both from the grassroots levels and from the policy levels at the very top. He continued with various assignments for the next three years, travelling to different countries and understanding people's issues, knowing at the back of his mind that cinema was where his future eventually lay.

> Kamal remains responsive and open-minded to the opportunities and resources available to him, using his strengths to leverage these towards reaching his dream.

Through different assignments in different countries, he also established a network with cinema producers and directors, working with them during his spare time, learning the ropes. His passion stood out and word about him spread.

Then one day, one of the biggest movie directors in India got in touch with him, offering Kamal an opportunity to assist him on an important movie that would change the way audiences looked at the issue of prostitution.

Kamal's decision was clear—he resigned from his highly paying job and joined the director in pursuit of his lifelong dream.

Need we guess how his life would pan out in the future?

Behind the Scenes

This real-life story of Kamal encompasses all the elements of self-awareness. The starting point of Kamal's success is his insight, self-knowledge and passion, which help him drive his life towards what he seeks. So why is it that so few individuals are able to achieve this self-actualisation? Family plays a big part in shaping individual identity in Indian culture. However, often the dilemma of balancing interdependence on and independence from family poses a challenge for individuals.

Knowing what we want and who we are as well as understanding the information our feelings tell us constitute one part of self-awareness; however, self-acceptance and taking accountability are equally critical. Society, our significant relationships and our circumstances all play a role in the choices we make. The answer is not that compromises need to be made necessarily, but differences need to be balanced and managed with empathy and care, while not letting go of our own passion. The constant connect with feelings and self enables the process of staying positive and ensuring focus, while being objective is all about 'reading the cues as they exist' and being realistic in our assessments.

In this story, Kamal knew where he was headed and the resources that were available to him. Knowledge of his inner strengths and self-conviction helped him keep his eye on the goal, despite changing circumstances. He was not afraid to leave a steady job in pursuit of his lifelong dream as he was certain that being a director is what would make him content. If he had been unsure of himself, he may have been led down a path that he was unsure of. His high self-appraisal abilities enabled him to make the most of the opportunities that came his way and ultimately realise his dream of becoming a director.

TOOLBOX Appraise Your Strengths and Weaknesses

Identify in your life significant times when you were successful and times when you experienced failures.

Successful events	The key strengths I used to create these successes	Not so successful events	The key weaknesses that could have led to these events

What are some of my internal drivers?	My behaviour-related profile (Behaviours that help me and behaviours that are unhelpful.)

'Your visions will become clear only when you can look into your own heart. Who looks outside, dreams; who looks inside, awakes.'

~ Carl Jung

SCENE 2

Recognising Your Reflection

Emotional Self-awareness

'Unless you learn what makes you tick and how your personal style affects you in every situation, you have no chance of controlling your behaviour, let alone preventing your emotions from controlling you. But when you know yourself, your core features, your strengths and weaknesses, your boundaries and breaking points, you can develop strategies to prevent going over the edge.'

~ Prashnig B.

MEETA'S STORY: OVERCOMING YOUR PERSONAL DEMONS

Meeta walked out of her boss's office in a daze. The long years that had led up to this moment played out in a flashback…

At the age of 23, Meeta jumped for joy when she landed a job at an international consulting firm. She had just completed her MBA and was eager to explore this opportunity to learn and challenge herself. It was also a chance to prove her worth. Subsequently, she worked long hours and travelled extensively but enjoyed every bit of it.

When she was 25, she was married to Jatin, the son of her father's friend, who worked as an associate consultant in a leading MNC. Unfortunately, it did not take Meeta long to realise that Jatin was highly insecure. Whenever she was late getting back from work, he would fly into a rage. And it was not just that; he had an issue with everything—the time she spent with her friends, her inability to answer the phone when he called her at work and so on. She tried to put his fears to rest, and when that did not work, she told herself that she needed to handle the situation better. Perhaps she was overreacting because of her high-stress job.

> Being in touch with your emotions instead of trying to suppress or deny them is an integral part of emotional self-awareness. It takes courage and self-honesty to recognise what is really bothering you, and then to deal with it effectively.

Then one day, Meeta discovered that Jatin was cheating on her. Her world came crashing down. She locked herself in her bathroom for an hour and replayed the events in her head. Finally, she decided she would not confront him with this discovery just yet. She thought about speaking to a friend, but was too ashamed.

> Take a moment and think about what you would do if you were in Meeta's situation. Would you do anything differently? How so? Why?

She walked into the office the next day with a severe headache; she had barely slept a wink all night. Her papers for the 10 a.m. meeting with the country head were not in place, and she found herself uneasy and fretful. Although she managed to get the right papers, the meeting was a disaster as she was not adequately prepared. For the rest of the day, she drowned herself in work and concentrated on the growing piles of paper on her desk and on trying to meet the deadlines. Upon reaching home, she hit the bed without waiting to have dinner. Despite her fatigue, she found it hard to sleep and kept tossing and turning all night.

This went on for several days. Challenging work that she had once looked forward to now seemed impossible to cope with. Back home, it was another sleepless night. She kept blaming work for causing this high level of anxiety. One day, exhausted beyond words and unable to sleep, she finally helped herself to some sleeping pills in the wee hours of the morning. She told a seemingly concerned Jatin that work had been pulling her down lately and that all the pressure in her office had made her sick.

For the next two weeks, Meeta developed a fever and just did not feel well enough to be back at work. Each night, she took some more pills and rested—feeling very frail and weak. There were endless visits to the doctor, but they all said the same thing—her illness was 'idiopathic', that is, arising from unknown causes. She figured that she was extremely over-worked and the stress was responsible for her low immunity.

> To be able to confront and deal with your personal demons, you have to be aware of them. Pay special note to how Meeta attributes her deteriorating health and work performance on everything but the real cause.

The fever continued, but Meeta could not stay away from work any longer. At office, she faced mounting pressure and seemingly impossible deadlines. The next few days saw her struggle to keep up. She would stay up late to complete the pending work, which would hamper her ability to function the next day. This would mean more work to take home the next day...and so the vicious cycle continued. Things slowly got worse; Meeta could no longer take the long hours in office and her previously impeccable research now had glaring flaws in it. Meetings, reports or deadlines slipped her mind, despite several reminders. She always had a slight fever, a headache or a perennial cold to blame for her mistakes or oversight and would often find herself at the brink of tears when someone spoke harshly to her.

Her boss finally decided to take her aside to discuss matters with her. After a lengthy discussion, he let her go with a warning. However, her performance continued to drop, and she was absent more often than not. After three months of continued negligence, impromptu leaves and random emotional outbursts, she was asked to leave the firm.

Meeta walked out of her boss's office in a daze, unable to believe that despite working so hard for the past three years, she had been laid off.

She returned home to an irritated Jatin who did not take the news of being the sole breadwinner well. When Meeta confronted him with the fact that he was cheating on her, the situation worsened. Jatin lost his cool, blamed her for their marriage falling apart and asked her to leave the house.

> Not dealing with your emotions in a timely manner can have far-reaching implications, affecting every aspect of your life. The longer you suppress your feelings, the more these implications intensify and spiral out of control.

Meeta felt a surprising sense of calm as she packed her things to move to her parents' house.

After weeks of confinement, Meeta agreed to see a friend for a cup of coffee. It was while she was speaking to her about her new-found calm that Meeta finally realised something crucial: it had been Jatin—and not work—that had caused her immense anxiety and stress all along.

Gradually, with her friend's encouragement, Meeta joined a non-governmental organisation (NGO) and became involved in teaching underprivileged children while she looked for a full-time job. She did not realise how much she enjoyed it until she found herself going to the NGO even on Sundays.

Meeta had never felt so free and full of life before. She was discovering new things about herself as she worked with the children. With the extra time on her hands, Meeta spent time introspecting and exploring her feelings. She tried to understand why she felt the way she did. A friend recommended blogging as a way to express herself, and she was touched by the generous comments her blog received from her friends and family. While she enjoyed the NGO work, she knew she wanted to go back to the consulting world soon. With some effort, she found a job at a small firm in her city. Meeta was determined to make the most of this opportunity. This time round, there was no looking back...

> Pay special note to the role friends and family play in Meeta's journey towards emotional self-awareness and fulfilment. This network can be an invaluable tool towards self-reflection, as well as a source of strength and inspiration in helping you overcome any emotional challenges and recreate your life.

Three years and two promotions later, Meeta was steadily climbing the ladder of success. She was known to be a calm and poised professional who rarely lost her temper, driving performance through motivation and encouragement instead. Every day, she pushed herself to become more self-aware and to manage her emotions well. Her new self was confident, in control and willing to laugh and experiment. But most of all, Meeta was comfortable in her own skin because she now knew how to read her emotions and where she was coming from.

Behind the Scenes

Meeta's story highlights the importance of knowing the cause of your feelings early on, so you can manage the situation better. This happens when you are in touch with your emotions and understand when and why they intensify. Meeta attributed her ill health and mental exhaustion to the pressures at work, not willing to accept that it was actually marital stress that was at the root of all her problems. She was also unable and unwilling to confront the issues with Jatin as they cropped up. It was only when her marriage ended that she got a new chance at life. Emerging from her shell gave her a chance to explore herself better. Her personal victories had a direct bearing on her professional progress. After years of an oppressed and gloomy life, Meeta learned to recognise the cause of her anxiety and the importance of actively dealing with real problems rather than ignoring them.

So often, while going through life, we externalise problems and fail to understand or confront ourselves. This in turn creates dramas in which we, our families and our friends remain entangled for years. Wouldn't it be better if we could turn the mirror inwards? If we could use emotions to understand our deep needs, desires, fears and patterns? By building insights into our reactions and behaviours and directing this understanding into creating situations that we want, we feel more confident, in control and fulfilled.

TOOLBOX   Understanding Your Emotions

Reflect back to the situations of successes that you identified in the earlier section.

Positive emotions that you experienced	Triggers that caused these emotions (What, in the situation, made you feel like this?)	What were your bodily sensations and responses when you experienced these positive emotions?

Reflect back to the situations of failure that you identified in the earlier section.

Negative emotions that you experienced	Triggers that caused these emotions (What, in the situation, made you feel like this?)	What were your bodily sensations and responses when you experienced these negative emotions?

TIPS AND TRICKS   Identifying the Root Cause

Getting in touch with your emotions is not always easy. Here is one simple way of getting to the root of what you are feeling. It is called the 'five whys' method. Using Meeta's story as an example, here is how the method works:

Meeta: I have a bad headache today.
Why?
Meeta: Because I didn't sleep well last night.
Why?
Meeta: Because I was feeling stressed by all the work I still have to do for the office.
Why?
Meeta: Because I have been unable to concentrate on my job and my work is slipping.
Why?
Meeta: Because my mind is distracted.
Why?
Meeta: Because my home situation is bad and I don't know how to deal with it, and I feel stuck and miserable.

Now you try it. Think of a situation where you have been feeling stressed and ask yourself five 'whys' until you get to the root of your problem.

Recognising and understanding your emotions is an important step towards emotional self-awareness. Once you are aware of your emotions, it becomes easier to manage them—but only if you adopt an objective approach. In the next section, we explore the concept of 'objectivity' through Sahil's story.

SCENE 3

Getting in Sync with Reality

Objectivity

'I must try to see the difference between my picture of a person and his behavior ... and the person's reality as it exists regardless of my interests, needs and fears.'

~ Erich Fromm

SAHIL'S STORY: GETTING STUCK IN YOUR OWN MIND

At Kwatra Foods, profits depended heavily on exports to other parts of the world; therefore, the global recession hit them heavily. Within weeks, they lost two key clients who accounted for almost 40 per cent of their revenue. In these dire circumstances, Kwatra Foods decided it would be best to cut down on their staff. Clearly, with two key clients gone, the company no longer needed as many hands on board. At such a time, costs needed to be managed to sustain the organisation. Hence, low performers were asked to leave and the others were encouraged to take up multiple roles. Raising the performance benchmark was another way to check promotions and, consequently, higher salaries.

However, many people revolted against the new policy. Sahil, a senior project manager in the R&D division, was one such employee. He was taken aback and very upset when he was informed that his team member Mohit was not going to meet the performance benchmark.

> Objectivity involves 'tuning in' to the immediate situation and keeping things in the correct perspective without excessive fantasising. Pay special note to how Sahil gets caught up in his own thoughts, allowing no room for external perspectives.

During the half-yearly appraisal a few months ago, Mohit, a quiet but hardworking team player, was rated 2.5/5 on his performance. He had been put on a performance improvement plan, and Sahil had actively coached him to get better results. Mohit had worked very hard under Sahil's guidance. He voluntarily attended two training programmes, read several books and articles that were recommended, sought feedback from his team and made several changes in the way he worked. Mohit also proactively took on an independent stretch target to develop himself.

Sahil carefully monitored Mohit's performance, reviewing it regularly. There was an evident shift in Mohit's performance, and the whole team was proud of his efforts. Sahil was set to give him a 4/5 this time around when he was told about the new rating system by the human resources (HR)— the performance benchmark had been raised across the company for all roles. As per the new system, people would be rated a score of 0.5 less than what they would have for the same level of performance. This meant Sahil would now have to give Mohit an overall score of 3.5/5. This meant Mohit would not be due for a promotion, as the criteria for promotions had also been revised.

> Sahil has clearly become attached to Mohit over the past few months, forming a close 'mentor–mentee'-style relationship. This makes it hard for him to assess the situation objectively and align with the new company policy. An important aspect of objectivity is the degree of clarity with regard to your thoughts and emotions.

For the past few months, Sahil had been praising Mohit's efforts to the skies and had even hinted at a move up the ladder. Now, how could he possibly tell Mohit that his performance had gone up by one mark only and that there would be no promotion? It was unfair that the company expected Mohit to suffer for their loss. Sahil was in a tight spot now and did not know how to deal with it. He felt miserable and disagreed vehemently with the management's decision.

'Organisations are ruthless and self-serving,' he thought to himself. 'They are always "all about money". This is terrible—Mohit will lose faith in me forever. I cannot bear to be the one to make him cynical in life.' Such repeated 'self-dialogues' made it impossible for Sahil to convey the bad news.

> Sahil's lack of awareness in discerning between his personal perceptions and what is happening on the ground leads him to make dramatic assumptions about how Mohit will be affected. You need to be aware of your emotions and have your feet firmly planted in reality. Objective people depend on facts to confirm and validate feelings and thoughts. This helps them navigate tough situations in a rational manner.

Sahil decided to speak to his manager about this development. His boss explained the company strategy and the reason behind the new performance system. While Sahil understood the rationale of the decision, he was not convinced that it was the right move. Not getting the answer he was looking for, he turned to HR for help. The HR manager had been expecting such concerns and gave Sahil useful tips on how to have the conversation with Mohit. However, Sahil was still not satisfied. What he really wanted was a way to reverse the scores.

He spent the next day pondering on the issue deeply. He felt the entire situation was terribly unfair to Mohit. HR did not know how hard Mohit had worked or how much he had stretched himself. And Sahil, knowing that, felt he could not possibly tell Mohit that he was not going to be promoted. After much deliberation, Sahil decided not to go to work the next morning and face the situation that he now saw as impossibly hard. He sent in his resignation over email, ending his dilemma once and for all.

Behind the Scenes

Sahil's real-life story demonstrates how a lack of objectivity can cause serious stress and have ramifications on one's career. Objectivity is the ability to assess the correspondence between what is subjectively experienced and what objectively exists. Once we are aware of our emotions, it becomes easier to manage them—but only if we adopt an objective approach.

Our lack of awareness and the resulting assumptions can pull us into all kinds of unnecessary dramas. We assume, for example, that when love is shared with another, there is none left for us. We assume that if things do not happen exactly as we want them to, it is totally awful and unacceptable. We assume that there can never be another perspective to what we call values or behaviours—instead of assessing our own thoughts, feelings and biases, we ascribe motives and pronounce judgements on others.

Sahil became inextricably caught up in his own thoughts: *Mohit will* never *trust again*, and *he (Sahil) would be the cause of this*. His paradigm about the *organisation being ruthless* did not help either. These strong assumptions caused Sahil such deep internal disturbance and stress that he chose to quit rather than speak to Mohit.

Could the drama have played out differently? If Sahil had accurately assessed the situation, he would have probably realised that he had become extremely attached to Mohit, as he had been guiding him and seeing him work hard over the past few months. This had clouded his ability to accept and convey the news. Sahil also made many assumptions about how Mohit would react without actively checking with him.

Perhaps Mohit would have understood the situation; perhaps he would have appreciated Sahil's concern and accepted the fact that the recession had created unavoidable circumstances with regard to promotions; perhaps he would have been glad to still have a job at a time when people were getting laid off. But Sahil, stuck in the melodrama in his head, never gave any of these possibilities a chance. At the end of the day, his decision accomplished nothing. Obviously, Mohit still would not get a promotion, and Sahil wound up derailing his career at the worst possible time—during a global financial crisis.

In philosophy, a statement is considered to be objectively true when it is free of a person's own feelings, beliefs or judgements and hence can be thought of as 'mind-independent'. In the emotional world, it is impossible for facts to be mind-independent, but it is possible for them to be realistic. It is important for us to strike a balance in our views, ensuring fairness and accuracy of facts.

> 'Buddhism is neither pessimistic nor optimistic. If anything at all, it is realistic, for it takes a realistic view of life and the world. It looks at things objectively (yathābhūtam)...It tells you exactly and objectively what you are and what the world around you is, and shows you the way to perfect freedom, peace, tranquility and happiness.'
>
> ~ Walpola Rahula

TOOLBOX A Reality Check for Your Thoughts and Feelings

Think of a situation that you are in currently or a decision that you have to make. The situation is one in which you are anxious of the outcome or the impact on other people or yourself.

List down your feelings	List down the facts	Get someone else's view	Make a decision

---

TOOLBOX   'ABCDE'[1]

Think of an upsetting situation you have experienced over the past week. In Column C (consequence), write down what your unpleasant feelings were and what behaviours accompanied them.

1. Write down the incident—the activating event—that seemed to trigger this upsetting situation in Column A.
2. The key aspect of the ABCDE approach is to now capture your Bs: that almost imperceptible, easily overlooked self-talk triggered by the activating event. See if you can pin down what went on in your mind right after the activating event. Change the above few lines.

---

[1] Adapted from Steven J. Stein and Howard E. Book, 2006, *The EQ Edge*, Canada: Stoddart Publishing Co. Ltd.

3. Your next task is to actively debate, dispute and discard (D) these maladaptive, self-defeating beliefs that give rise to your Cs. Submit every element of your internal monologue to rigorous examination. Ask yourself the following key questions and write down your answers in Column D:

   a. *Where is the proof?*
   b. *Are there alternative, more logical explanations, to explain the activating event?*
   c. *If someone asked me for advice about this scenario, what might I say that could help alter his/her perspective?*

4. Finally, in Column E, write down the effects of filling in Column D—how debating, disputing and discarding have shifted your understanding and beliefs about the activating event and, consequently, your feelings and behaviours.

A	B	C	D	E

Know More: Faulty Assumptions, Global Consequences

An industry-wide lack of objectivity can have dangerous results that impact millions of people. The U.S. housing bust, combined with the downfall of Lehman Brothers in 2007–2008, which triggered a shocking global recession, was built on the foundation of a large number of faulty assumptions:

1. *Real estate values constantly increase.* Assuming that home values would keep going up was a catastrophic miscalculation—for Citigroup, Merrill Lynch, Fannie Mae and countless homeowners.
2. *There will always be a buyer.* When home values started to fall, nobody wanted to invest heavily in an asset that could be worthless the next day.
3. *Banks are consistently responsible with their money.* We all know how that turned out.
4. *Do not worry, technology will save us.* Wall Street's massive electronic network enables millions of global transactions each day. But the traders could not track the risk, and the situation spun out of control quickly. Lightning-fast computers ended up endangering the entire system.
5. *The government will save us.* There are clearly limitations to government action.
6. *This cannot happen here and now.* The massive, widespread recession reminded us that business cycles are very much a thing of the present.

Source: Adapted from http://money.usnews.com/money/blogs/flowchart/2008/12/15/the-10-worst-assumptions-of-2008

Becoming Your Own Best Friend

Self-expression

'Unexpressed emotions will never die. They are buried alive and will come forth later in uglier ways.'

~ Sigmund Freud

AKANSHA'S STORY: THE POWER OF EXPRESSING YOURSELF

An expert at data warehousing and managing a team of four, Akansha was a senior software engineer at Premium Logic, a leading information technology (IT) firm. She was quiet, polite and likeable. Although she took her time to open up to people, she got along with everyone.

On the personal front, Akansha had been feeling some resentment towards her in-laws. While they treated her well and were nice to her, she sometimes felt they took her for granted. For instance, often her husband and in-laws (with whom she lived) assumed that she would cook special food for their friends or go out shopping with them whenever they asked her. Akansha never said no—despite the resentment she felt simmering under the surface, which was slowly turning into rage.

> Self-expression is the ability to express emotions, beliefs and thoughts and to defend our rights in an assertive and non-destructive manner.
>
> This behaviour becomes extremely critical, especially in interpersonal situations such as the one Akansha is facing.

On the work front, Akansha's manager had given her feedback for the low performance of her team. She had been feeling the heat ever since. The more she thought about it, the more confused and helpless she felt about how to take things forward.

One morning, while Akansha was getting dressed for office, her husband told her that he had booked tickets for an evening movie. Before she knew it, she started yelling at him, saying that he should not have assumed she would be free as she had a lot on her plate. She had already made plans to go out with her friends that evening. He responded saying that it was no big deal; they could always cancel the tickets and go another time. But Akansha was unable to calm down, and she continued screaming at him for not checking with her first. He was taken aback by this sudden outburst, and after a few failed attempts at diffusing her anger, he accused her of being crazy when she stormed out of the house. Akansha knew her reaction had been out of proportion and felt uncomfortable—she was not at peace.

> Akansha's overreaction is due to her failure to confront—not only her own emotions but also other's actions. When we consistently fail to confront issues, the predictable results are (a) feeling that our needs have not been met, (b) high levels of resentment and (c) cumulative damage to the relationship.

In her following performance review, the manager found that the team's performance had not improved. On probing, he found that Akansha had avoided speaking to her team members about their performance, which was one of her actions post her last review. Instead, she was trying to take on more work, which in turn was causing her stress and not enhancing the performance of her team. Akansha's manager realised that she had difficulties in having open conversations with her team about their poor performance. Post her agreement, he enrolled her for a training workshop on emotional intelligence.

> To express one's own views often requires some kind of confrontation, but the mere idea of confronting someone arouses certain negative feelings in Akansha. She is afraid to confront because she is afraid of dealing with these feelings, even if the other's actions are unacceptable to her.

Akansha was unsure of what to expect from the workshop. While going through the workshop, she understood her own limitations of being able to deal with the fear that struck her every time she went through conflicts. She recognised how this fear impacted her and her relationships. She learned techniques to manage her feelings and gained tools to structure her messages. Akansha observed other members expressing themselves effectively in the session and resolved to use her learning in defined situations at work and at home. Her action planning was clear and focused.

After the workshop, Akansha continued to work with the consultant, realising that what stopped her from expressing her views or needs was her belief that this would make others dislike her and she would become alienated. While helping her examine her belief, the consultant encouraged Akansha to test her belief by giving feedback to one of her team members.

> As leaders, we must be willing and able to confront effectively when the inevitable unacceptable behaviours of others occur. During interpersonal conflicts, the question to ask yourself is: 'Am I just uptight and crabby today? Or is this behaviour really unacceptable?'

Nervously, Akansha called in Ankur, one of the team members, for a discussion the next day. She started the conversation well, and proceeded to give facts on how he had not been proactive. In turn, she listened carefully to what he had to say in reply. While giving feedback, she attempted to be calm and composed, even though she could feel her anxiety rising on some occasions.

> Confrontation is always a request for change. Change is difficult and, thus, will always require some degree of courage.

Ankur was surprised when he heard what Akansha had to say. He told her that he had no clue that his manager felt this way about him for the past three months. He thanked her for sharing her feedback and shared his ideas of what he could do to improve. Together, they came up with a plan of action.

After the meeting, Akansha walked into her office and dropped into her chair. She relived the meeting, going through each little detail. She thought of what she had said and rephrased a few sentences in her head. Perhaps she could have created more impact if she had said a few things differently; however, somewhere deep within, she realised that she was extremely relieved and happy that she had taken this first step. The whole experience had been very stressful, after all, because speaking this way was new to her. However, Akansha also experienced pride and a sense of freedom for being able to say exactly what was on her mind. She resolved to continue practising her new-found skill at work and at home—recognising that change would not happen overnight.

Behind the Scenes

If we do not value ourselves, no one else will. A self-aware leader understands his/her needs, feelings and beliefs. An effective, self-aware manager, through the art of self-expression, succeeds in having his/her needs met without violating the needs and feelings of others. While going through interpersonal situations, differences and conflicts often appear, consequently causing uncomfortable feelings to surface. The complex process of managing internal conflicts—in Akansha's case, being well-liked versus meeting her needs or meeting her goals—starts with an awareness of these internal conflicts. From this awareness, one learns to manage these conflicts and to communicate or express oneself effectively.

The reason confrontation is so painful, and therefore usually avoided, is that we view confrontation as being unnecessarily blameful, controlling and punishing. It requires a high degree of awareness and self-confidence to be able to 'express ourselves' authentically and effectively. Contrast this with the many games we often play at work or elsewhere—speaking to everyone else rather than to the concerned person, communicating a difficult message apologetically or ambiguously and withdrawing/avoiding open communication. At other times, when we are overwhelmed with emotion, we express ourselves in a hurtful way without thinking about how our words will impact the other person. An example of this would be a manager, who is very angry at an order that has been lost, lashing out at his team member because his own target will not be met, without thought to the effort that the team member may have put into the order and how difficult it may have been for him to lose it. No wonder, building and sustaining deep and authentic relationships is no easy task!

TOOLBOX	Constructive Confrontation

Confrontation is inherently a part of self-expression. But it does not have to be destructive or disrespectful. Below is an exercise to help you work through ways to confront that are constructive for both you and the person you are confronting.

Think of an important conversation/meeting that you are due to have in the next week.

What is your view on the issue?	How will you express it?
	Voice message (Tone, etc.)
	Verbal message (Your 'I' message)*
	Body message
	Voice message (Tone, etc.)
	Verbal message (Your 'I' message)
	Body message

*Four Elements of an 'I-Message'

- *Observation*
  The concrete action/event I see, hear or remember ('... I didn't get what you promised ...')
- *Feeling*
  How this affects/ hits me ('... I am surprised ...')
- *Need*
  My unmet need in this situation ('... I want to avoid ...')
- *Request*
  ('... I would like you to ... next time')

SOME USEFUL PHRASES TO START 'I' MESSAGES OF NEEDS AND FEELINGS:

I want to be sure ....

I am relieved that I do not have to..

I want to avoid by all means...

I need more time..

I cannot accept..

I need to know before ....

I want to consider first...

I decided to...

I do not want to spend (more) time/money on ....

I am not really helped by your ....

I am afraid...

It took me by surprise that ....

I feel bad about ....

I am confused when ....

ACT 2   Lights! Camera! Action!

Are You Staying on Track?

Self-management

'The truth is that we can learn to condition our minds, bodies, and emotions to link pain or pleasure to whatever we choose. By changing what we link pain and pleasure to, we will instantly change our behaviours.'

~ Tony Robbins

INTRODUCTION TO SELF-MANAGEMENT

At critical junctures in our life, we are confronted with drastic changes, upheavals and other stressful situations in which we feel weighed down by the strong emotions that leap out at us. On a more micro-scale, when dealing with the hassles of daily living, we also experience a steady ebb and flow of emotions—stress, joy, anxiety, excitement, irritation and so on. The way we cope with these situations and emotions directly impacts our ability to function. If these emotions and situations are not handled well, they could derail us in our path towards our long-term goals.

Self-management and self-motivation are the two key factors that help keep our life on track, productive, and fulfilled.

In this chapter, we will explore the concept of self-management—the ability to manage one's emotions.

Quite simply, self-management is about being our own emotional 'remote control'. It is about being able to 'zap' to the most appropriate emotion on our 'emotional screen' — the one that best fits the situation, the one that creates the best results for ourselves as well as the people around us and the one that flexibly and effectively solves the problem at hand. This skill is not only about being able to handle negative emotions; it also includes the ability to respond to positive emotions such as passion and obsession.

Self-management is about creating a good balance between sense and sensibility, with effective ways to confront, understand and deal with the emotional ups and downs of life.

In this chapter, we will explore the five components of self-management:

- *Stress-management*: Actively coping with adverse events and stressful situations.
- *Impulse control*: Controlling disruptive emotions and impulses.
- *Self-reliance*: Being independent in one's thinking and behaviour.
- *Adaptability*: Being flexible and willing to change.
- *Problem-solving*: Generating and implementing potentially effective solutions to daily problems.

Each of these components will be illustrated through stories of people dealing with self-management issues in their everyday life. The stories will be followed by exercises that help you tangibly apply the concept of self-management to your particular experiences and situation.

'A man is but the product of his thoughts. What he thinks, he becomes.'

~ Mahatma Gandhi

SCENE 1

Taking a Deep Breath

Stress-management

'Stress is an important dragon to slay—or at least tame—in your life.'

~ Marilu Henner

PRASHANT'S STORY: BEING HANDICAPPED BY STRESS

When Prashant broke the news to his father of his decision to move to yet another organisation, his father could not help but be disappointed. This was Prashant's fifth move in three years.

A topper from a premier business school and an alumnus of one of the country's leading engineering colleges, Prashant had risen to a leadership position in the short span of two years. However, he could not stick to a job for more than a few months. As a result, his career was not progressing. With every job switch, he would inevitably spend a certain period of time settling down in the new workplace and building credibility; by the time these elements were in place, he would want out.

His father could not understand his son's apparent flippancy with jobs, especially since he himself had worked in one organisation for nearly 30 years. He felt that working in one organisation helped him to add value in many different areas. When he finally retired, he felt that he had truly left his mark in his company. Prashant, however, would just be another brick in the wall if he continued down this path. Overcome with worry, Prashant's father decided to have a heart-to-heart discussion with him. That is when he discovered the root cause of Prashant's actions. It was stress.

> While every leader's handbook talks about stress and details tips on how to handle it, stress continues to thrive in people the world over. It can often cause us to make rash decisions and poor judgements. Each person has different stress triggers—notice how Prashant's feelings of worry and apprehension come about.

Prashant was a hard-worker and worked well as an individual contributor. Problems started arising when he first took on a position of leadership. When faced with a tough situation (and there were many), feelings of apprehension and fear would engulf Prashant. As long as there was a subordinate or a superior on the scene to handle the situation, or he could put off the decision, he was fine. However, as a leader, Prashant was often put in a position where he was required to take quick decisions in tough situations, where his decision could affect the fate of his team. Each time such a situation came up, Prashant would feel his throat become dry and his palms sweaty. He would continually pace up and down the room and avoid taking phone calls. He would feel buried under the weight of the decision, and with his mind on overdrive, he felt completely incapable of taking a stance. Eventually, he would feign sickness or escape the situation on some other pretext. This meant the task either would not get done or would be handed over to the second in command.

> You need to develop a healthy perspective about issues at the workplace. In Prashant's mind, coping with any difficult situation becomes a Herculean task.

Afterwards, Prashant would become extremely anxious, worrying about how others might react when they discovered this weakness. He would convince himself that his supervisors would scold him, while his team members would laugh at their incompetent boss. He would begin to doubt if he was fit for the job that had been handed to him. In this state of extreme stress, Prashant would look for the first job he could find before the company could ask him to leave because of his handicap. At the next job, this scenario would repeat itself again. And so on and so forth. At one company, Prashant's supervisor even tried to speak to him about this issue, but Prashant was unwilling to discuss it.

> The first step to dealing with an issue is to acknowledge it. Prashant's unwillingness to address his stress problem with his colleagues takes away the possibility of getting help. We must open ourselves to discussion and suggestions.

His father listened to his son and thought back to Prashant's childhood days, when he had sometimes missed school on weekly test days and had occasionally 'fallen sick' right before a crucial exam. He realised now where the problem lay. His son was carrying the heavy burden of debilitating, constant stress on his shoulders.

Behind the Scenes

Prashant, a bright young man with a promising future, is repeatedly derailed by his inability to cope with stress. Each of us has felt this nagging sense of worry and panic at some point in our lives—perhaps when faced with public speaking, while giving a board/entrance exam, during an interview or when workplace pressures and deadlines threaten our equilibrium.

With increasing competition, and in the current environment of quick changes, the capability to deal with difficult situations without getting overwhelmed is a desirable quality in managers and corporate leaders. It involves a fair amount of self-discipline that allows us to stay on a task and see it through in spite of the challenges along the way. Prashant, unfortunately, would lose his focus on the work problem itself, instead getting inundated by his fears and feelings about the *process* and *aftermath* of making a decision. He was unable to approach the problem by thinking, 'Okay, here's a problem. Let me solve it and move on to other things.'

Difficulty in managing stress often leads to anxiety with symptoms such as irritability, tension, disturbed sleep, poor concentration and indecisiveness. These symptoms can take a toll on our overall ability to function at home and at work. We do need a certain amount of stress in order to function and do our best. However, as with most things, too much stress can cause problems. The point is not to avoid stress, but to learn to manage and use it positively.

TOOLBOX   Slaying the Stress Dragon

There are a number of tools and lifestyle changes that can help you deal with stress at the workplace—or even in your personal life.

List the things, people, situations that are stressful. Write down why they are stressful.	
Be aware of what happens physically and mentally when you feel stressed. Identify your stress signals.	
Identify your stress management techniques such as relaxation techniques, physical exercise, life style management and time management.	
How will you apply these? And whose help will you need?	

> 'Nothing can stop the man with the right mental attitude from achieving his goal; nothing on earth can help the man with the wrong mental attitude.'
>
> ~ Thomas Jefferson

AAMIR'S STORY: DEALING WITH THE CATCH-22 OF STRESS

Aamir, a project manager at a premium multinational IT company, had a job that involved the delivery of technology projects of varying complexity. He was a talented resource who was known as a technical guru in the organisation, and his expertise and dedication to excellence had rapidly pushed him up the ladder.

A typical workday in Aamir's life began at 8 a.m. sharp. He started the day by checking his mail and deciding his priorities for the day. Within an hour, Aamir could be seen shuffling between multiple tasks and meetings, making sure that the quality of the team's outputs was par excellence. The key challenges of his role were:

1. Keeping the team motivated.
2. Managing multiple, geographically distributed clients.
3. Diffusing crisis situations as and when they arose.

All these challenges could be a source of stress and anxiety, more so for Aamir as he was a perfectionist. He had set the bar high for himself and for his team. He was very particular about ensuring the quality of any output. He often spent large amounts of time reworking documents that his team members had produced to ensure that they met his personal quality standards. Despite starting his day early, Aamir could often be seen working late into the night. This aspect of his personality ensured that feelings of unease and apprehension were always at the surface. He was unhappy most of the time and knew this was because of stress. He had started to become quiet and withdrawn. He thought incessantly about work and factors that were beyond his control.

> In his quest for perfection and for maintaining his reputation, Aamir is unable to delegate work to his team members. This adds to his stress and creates problems for him personally and professionally.

During the monthly performance review, his manager highlighted that Aamir had been unable to complete his deliverables for the month. While the organisation was pleased with the quality he was delivering, he needed to work faster so he could manage everything on his plate.

Aamir was not surprised as he knew his own strengths and shortcomings well. In the last review, his manager had suggested that Aamir should empower his team and enable them to share his load. This would allow him to focus on some of the critical areas that were getting neglected. However, another month had passed and the manager had not seen any improvement. He asked what was holding Aamir back.

> While Aamir is self-aware enough to know his strengths and weaknesses, he is unable to translate this knowledge into an action plan to reduce stress and increase productivity.

Aamir knew that he should delegate more tasks, but the question remained: How? On further probing from his manager, he admitted that the problem was deeper than simply letting go of work. Every time he was to work on a critical project, he started to worry about the results before his work even began. His pulse rate rose with a million thoughts zooming through his head, and he stopped communicating. His thoughts turned to what could go wrong at each step.

Aamir constantly worried about living up to his reputation for excellence. He realised it was tough for him to step out of this trap.

The manager smiled as he asked Aamir to examine his beliefs. Was it true that everything would go wrong? Was it true that his reputation would be ruined? Aamir realised that his thoughts were not grounded in reality and he needed to think more constructively in stressful situations. He started to see the self-destructive patterns in his thoughts. Slowly, he was beginning to realise that the stress he had caused himself could, over time, stunt his professional growth. Yet, it was also because of the high quality of his outputs that he had been largely successful in his professional life. He needed to find a way to balance his stress levels with his obsession for perfection.

> Pay special note to the catch-22 situation Aamir finds himself in. It is important to focus on balance when coming up with strategies for stress management.

Aamir introduced a few stress-busting activities in his schedule, depending on when he got home from work—a half-hour walk regime, an hour's relaxation time, enjoying a leisurely cup of coffee or dinner with his family. It seemed odd to actually schedule time for relaxation; however, after trying it for a few days, he found that it was working. He also picked up a weekend hobby course on photography—something he had always wanted to do, but felt he never had the time for. At work, too, he made an effort to communicate more with his colleagues.

The true test of whether Aamir had made a change came five months later when there was a massive time crunch on one of the projects that he was assigned. He was aware of his tendency to feel stressed, so the moment he was put in charge of the project, he sat down with his team to create a plan. With a solid plan in place, his anxiety was temporarily alleviated. In the days to come, he felt the familiar feeling of his pulse racing and, at times, just wanted to shut himself up in a room. However, this time, Aamir made a conscious effort to keep his anxiety levels in check and his communication levels up. A number of issues came to the surface when he spoke to his team, and the early diagnosis ensured that the problems were sorted before they snowballed into something bigger. He noticed that his team members now approached him more often because he no longer alienated himself during a crisis. The project was a huge success, and there was positive feedback from the customers. Aamir was applauded for managing time and resources effectively without compromising on quality.

Aamir finally breathed a sigh of relief and readied himself for the next challenge.

Behind the Scenes

In this story, Aamir's technical expertise in his field is what pushed him ahead at the start of his career. Later, this is also what stunted his growth. His reputation for being an expert drove him to be a perfectionist, and the high quality of his work helped him advance to a certain level in his career. However, despite leading a team of people who could assist him, Aamir often found himself getting sidetracked in mindless tasks, for example, reworking documents that his team members had created. This micro-management was an unnecessary source of pressure for him and detracted from his focus on critical tasks related to his role.

With the help of his manager, Aamir saw the need to change. While this was not easy, he pushed himself. Slowly and steadily, he found a balance between his personality and work demands. This allowed him to lead his team more effectively, overcome his own anxiety and create an environment that encouraged others to express themselves and do their best work.

TIPS AND TRICKS   Ways to Increase Work–Life Balance

Think back to your childhood summer vacations. What did you love to do during those long, wonderful holidays? Did you like playing sports with your friends, or did you love to read books, or watch movies, or spend time with your family? Was there a hobby you enjoyed—taking photographs, listening to music, learning to cook?

Whatever those things you loved doing when you were younger, find a way to incorporate them into your present-day life. Perhaps you could create a football or cricket group for weekends, or a book club. If you love cooking, perhaps you and your partner could cook a special meal together each week, or go for a 'date night'. Or else, you could tap into your city's cultural activities—movies, plays, musical events. These joys will not only enhance your mental well-being but also deeply enhance your work life and productivity.

Looking Before You Leap

Impulse Control

'Control your emotion or it will control you.'

~ Bertrand Russell

SHIV'S STORY: HARNESSING NEGATIVE IMPULSES

Shiv was often called a manufacturing guru. A creative and driven team leader, he had been leading five engineers in the Kanpur manufacturing plant of a beverages firm for the past two years and had seen much success in his early years. He dreamed big and was completely focused on meeting his goals, one way or another. His leadership philosophy was that people need to be pushed so they can discover their true potential; this led him to give his people stretch assignments and seemingly impossible targets.

In the pre-Diwali mayhem, Shiv's team was given a daily target of 100,000 units, although the plant's current production rate at the time stood at 72,000 units. Behind Shiv's back, the team jokingly dubbed this project 'Mission Impossible'. While not completely impossible to achieve, it was a massive stretch target and the whole team was working day and night to make it a reality. As Diwali drew nearer, the pressure on the team kept piling up. Shiv, too, was starting to feel the heat. Then, just a few days before Diwali, the dam broke.

As per department regulations, the team began each day with a meeting to share information, align on key tasks and discuss challenges. The agenda for that morning's meeting was more specific—one of Shiv's team members, Ajay, was responsible for a quality error the previous day that had led to a great deal of wastage.

Shiv brought this up in the morning meeting. Without giving Ajay a chance to explain, he began shouting at him loudly, ranting about his incompetence. 'Pull up your socks, or we won't be able to meet our goals!' he yelled. Shiv was accustomed to doing high-quality, timely work and could not tolerate mistakes from his team members. Moreover, he was a high performer, and he did not want to be pulled down by the incompetence of his team.

> When we are irritable and under stress, we are likely to get into a state where even a minor incident can release a volcanic eruption of rage. The minor provocation may be the proverbial straw that breaks the camel's back.

The next day, Ajay was caught in traffic and reached the plant an hour late. He tentatively walked into Shiv's office to explain the delay. The moment Shiv laid eyes on him, he lost his cool. He felt that despite the warning yesterday, Ajay was still not taking the matter seriously. Due to his irresponsible actions, the whole team would suffer.

The rest of the team could hear Shiv lashing out at Ajay. They realised he was in a bad mood again and decided to keep their distance from him the entire day. Shiv noticed this but shrugged it off as there were bigger things to worry about. He got back to the production chart and tried to devise a way to reconfigure the plan so they could meet their target. He spent the day barking out instructions to his team members in line with the new plan.

> Shiv is so caught up in his own stress and emotions that he does not realise the effect this is having on his team. Although he notices that the team is avoiding him, he is so involved in the task at hand that he ignores the warning signs.

The next week, Ajay approached Shiv's manager, Dipanjan, for a transfer. The reason he gave was that he could not keep up with the high-pressure environment in Shiv's team. He was willing to work hard and do well, but he felt that for Shiv, nothing he (Ajay) did would ever be good enough.

In light of this, Dipanjan called Shiv for a meeting to discuss Ajay's request. He explained that while Shiv was able to meet his numbers, that alone was not enough. To excel as a 'leader' in the true sense of the word, he needed to master the 'softer' aspects of management as well. He pointed out that how Ajay was not growing in his current role; he kept repeating the same mistakes and had now given up on trying to improve as he felt Shiv would pick on everything he did anyway.

Shiv was shocked to learn that one of his team members had actually asked for a transfer. Dipanjan also informed Shiv that most of his team members were growing increasingly demotivated and hesitated to approach Shiv directly, preferring to reach out to Dipanjan for solutions. Hurt and angry, Shiv began justifying his actions by listing the reasons for his behaviour—his team's low accountability, poor quality of work and how this ultimately impacted the customer. He told Dipanjan that he only scolded his team when they asked for it and that he believed he was equally generous with positive feedback, when they deserved it. Besides, despite some lapses, the team was performing reasonably well on the whole, meeting their targets most of the time, and even Dipanjan had seemed pleased with that.

Over the weekend, however, Shiv had an opportunity to introspect at a deeper level. Dipanjan's words echoed in his head. It suddenly struck Shiv that managing his emotions had been an issue for him for a long time. Plagued with this thought, he decided to work on improving himself and his interactions with others. He understood that if he did not change, he would not grow, either professionally or personally.

> Shiv is unable to deal with poor performance from anyone in his team. Although he feels he is reacting to the task at hand, some of his remarks are perceived as personal attacks. Dipanjan's feedback jolts Shiv out of his complacency. Notice how he tries to examine his own behaviour objectively.

Shiv went about this in a systematic way, and began by listing out the situations that tended to make him angry. He revisited the many past scenarios where he had vented his anger and thought of how it had affected the team. He recalled the team members he had scolded during high-pressure situations. As Dipanjan had suggested, he tried putting himself in Ajay's shoes—what must Ajay have felt when Shiv had shouted at him publicly? Shiv even compared his own management style to Dipanjan's. He realised that a common theme in his anger was his expectation from his team members that they *must always* perform like he does. He did not care about the reasons behind low performance and often lashed out without thinking of the impact it would have on the other person.

Reflecting on this, Shiv decided that the first step he would take henceforth in such situations would be to explore and ask questions around the gaps and reasons for the same. Asking questions would lead to two things. First, it would get the other person to talk through the problem, identifying gaps, if any, and taking more accountability. Second, it would give *him* an opportunity to think through as to *how* he would like to react. "This is what Dipanjan does so effectively—it is something that I can learn from him," he thought, making up his mind.

Five months later, at the annual off-site, Shiv, Ajay and the rest of his team stood on the podium, their faces lit up with broad smiles as they accepted an award for completing another Mission Impossible.

Behind the Scenes

Shiv was a high-performing individual but had difficulty being a good leader. Instead of addressing the problems in his team with a long-term approach, he would allow the pressure to build up and would then snap. This is what happened when Shiv lashed out at Ajay. Instead of scolding and berating his team members, Shiv could have used his expertise to coach the average team members to do better.

Impulse control is the practised ability to withstand strong emotions in stressful or adverse conditions, without losing our composure. If our emotions are in check, we have the confidence and the presence of mind to handle what comes our way.

Shiv had the awareness to eventually realise this fact. Despite his initial defensive reaction, his introspection shed light on what he was doing wrong. One of the great things about his new approach was the fact that he involved his team in his personal development, rather than keeping them at bay. Shiv grew sensitive to their reactions and feedback, and it was this quality that helped him learn which of his actions were received well and thus reinforced his positive behaviour.

This quality is essential for effective problem-solving and negotiation, as it prevents knee-jerk reactions and instead helps you read social cues and wait for the opportune moment. This is what leads to success in the long run. However, when you are unable to control your impulses, anger and frustration take control of you instead.

Remain calm, serene, always in command of yourself. You will then find out how easy it is to get along.'

~ Paramahansa Yogananda

CHAITANYA'S STORY: I WIN, EVERYBODY LOSES

In March 2000, a young entrepreneur Chaitanya, along with a team of five talented people, formed a small technology firm called MRF. The organisation grew steadily over the next decade. In 2011, the MRF team was approached by Tekram, a Malaysia-based company, for an investment opportunity in the company. This was the moment when MRF knew they had finally arrived.

After a month of meetings and negotiations, a final meeting was arranged at the Tekram headquarters. An official delegation from MRF flew to Malaysia to close the deal. The chief executive officers (CEOs) and chief financial officers (CFOs), valuation experts and top leaders from both sides were present. As the two teams presented their valuations, the air was rife with tension. As expected, the valuations differed and a discussion ensued, with each team trying to outshine the other. There was a constant volley of numbers and remarks being exchanged by the two teams, and while challenging the MRF team's perspective, the Tekram valuation expert made a technical faux pas.

Chaitanya, MRF's CEO, immediately noticed this and knew it would be the turning point in the negotiations. He excitedly pointed out the error, almost as if he had been waiting for the Tekram valuation expert to falter. The Tekram team was embarrassed and requested for some more time to recalibrate. However, having gained the upper hand, Chaitanya was unwilling to let go of this golden opportunity. He brought up the error repeatedly to underscore their expertise and superiority in their field.

The CEO of Tekram reluctantly agreed to work on MRF's terms. The Indian delegation was overjoyed and celebrated the night away. Meanwhile, the Tekram valuation expert went home seething. She was embarrassed at having lost face and angry that Chaitanya had continued to stress on her mistake and use it to his advantage. She was an ambitious person and hoped to progress rapidly. Her presence at this crucial meeting had been a clear indication that her CFO had faith in her. After this fiasco, however, he had pulled her aside to tell her that he was disappointed in her. She was enraged and vowed to make the Indian team pay for this.

In an unfortunate turn of events for the MRF team, she was their point of contact as part of the board of the company. Using this position, she turned her focus on bringing out operational flaws in the company rather than focusing on strategic issues. Over the months, other board members at Tekram came to believe that MRF was a bad investment.

Fraught with difficulties from the start, the deal eventually fell apart a year into the association.

Behind the Scenes

The above story illustrates how lack of impulse control on the part of Chaitanya at a critical moment led to problems in the partnership, eventually resulting in a dramatic split. Had he managed his emotions better, the MRF CEO would have been able to avoid making a personal attack on the Tekram valuation expert and established his expertise quietly instead. The Tekram expert's response was equally immature. She could have admitted her mistake and moved on.

A difficult relationship with a vendor puts pressure on both parties, and in this case, it also prevented Tekram from maximising the value they could have derived from the vendor, finally losing the deal altogether. Rather than being a win–win situation for both parties, the end result was a lost opportunity for both organisations.

TOOLBOX   Develop Your Impulse Control

1. Describe the event that triggered your anger/impulse and how you responded.

2. Give a synonym for your anger/impulse level (furious, annoyed, desperate, etc.) and rate your anger on a scale of 1 to 10.

3. What were the first symptoms of your anger/impulse—how did you first notice you were angry?

   a. Thoughts/judgements
   b. Body sensations

4. What were the underlying emotions that you felt?

5. What factors/beliefs do you think made you prone to act on your impulse in this situation?

6. What would you like to do next time?

7. Was the situation so important that you lost control of yourself?

8. What can you do to keep a check on yourself?

9. What can you do to not impact others negatively?

SCENE 3

Believing in Yourself

RAVI'S STORY: TRANSFORMING DREAMS INTO REALITY

After the Partition of India in 1947, Ravi came to Delhi with only a few rupees in his wallet. A landlord's son in Pakistan, a pauper in India: Ravi's early story echoes the situation of thousands of people who lived through the horror of the Partition. What makes his tale stand apart is that he was able to overcome the odds to become a name to reckon with in the field of construction and real estate development.

Ravi started his career in India as a clerk with a construction company in 1948, facing strong disapproval from his relatives. They felt that he should have started his own venture—that was the proper thing for someone from his background to do. They were also upset that he had joined a construction firm of all things. But Ravi was not deterred by their remarks. Construction fascinated him, and he wanted to learn the nuts and bolts of the business. Besides, his major concern at this stage was to have a fixed source of income that would take care of the basic needs of the family, especially his old mother.

In order to manage yourself, it is important to stand on your own feet and be independent in your thinking and actions. This allows you to function independently and to be free of emotional dependency. Ravi clearly believes in his own judgements despite being advised by friends and family to follow the conventional path.

From the very beginning, Ravi got actively involved in all aspects of the business. He worked for long hours in the office, understanding the challenges and the strategies of his employers to mitigate risks and earn profits from each venture. As the business grew, Ravi slowly climbed up the professional ladder and finally landed the opportunity to work as a business manager with the firm. His hard work and determination had paid off.

A few years later, Ravi's relatives urged him to marry Geeta, the only daughter of a restaurateur. They were keen for him to take the reins of her father's restaurant. While Ravi liked Geeta, he was not keen on joining her father's business. After much persuasion from his mother, he agreed to marry Geeta on the condition that he would not be pressured to carry forward the restaurant business. Ravi knew that his passion lay in construction and that one day he would start his own company.

People who rely on themselves rarely lean on others to make decisions for them, or do things for them. Ravi displays a sense of self-confidence and inner strength. Pay special note to how he is able to take initiative and complete tasks without relying excessively on help or approval from others.

The years soon after his marriage were tough on Ravi. The company he was working in suffered huge losses since the land that they were using turned out to be forest land that they were forced to return to the forest authorities, after a court order. The company's new projects also failed to take off due to increased competition and also due to differences amongst the owners. The company finally closed down and Ravi lost his job.

Ravi was extremely worried as he now had the added responsibility of supporting his wife and new baby. Seeing no other way out of the situation, he began to work in his father-in-law's restaurant, much to the joy of his family, who thought that it was a blessing in disguise. Ravi never gave up the idea of having his own construction company, and when one of his friends approached him to float a joint construction venture, he readily accepted the offer. They started with small jobs and government contracts on road construction, repair of school buildings, dilapidated buildings, subcontracted jobs and so on. They worked hard together, and Ravi's experience came in handy. The good relationships he had built with government authorities in the past helped him get more work.

> Ravi focuses on co-operation and interdependence in the business world—rather than dependence.

Ravi's first big contract came in 1965. By this time, his partner had left him for more lucrative opportunities in garment export. He had tried his best to persuade Ravi to abandon the construction business and join him in his new venture, but Ravi stuck to his guns and floated his own company Om Constructions. Steadily, he built his company up, capitalising on every opportunity that came his way and accepting every failure as a learning experience.

Ravi worked hard to raise capital for his business from private moneylenders and from financial institutions. The residential complex that he built in 1968 for the middle-income group became a huge hit. There was no looking back after that: luxury homes, high-rise apartments, farmhouses, holiday homes, commercial buildings, offices, hotels and so on. By 2010, Om Constructions had successfully invaded every sphere of the construction business.

Even though everyone else is opposed to it, Ravi stands on his own feet and pursues his dream with total dedication. He is an independent thinker and relies first and foremost on his own judgement. Yet, he also has the self-awareness and self-confidence to be co-operative and adaptable.

During this period, Ravi worked with some of the best professionals in the country; he shared his vision with them and also empowered them to try new business ideas. Soon, he listed his company on the National Stock Exchange.

Today, Om Constructions has more than 10,000 employees, with offices across India and in Dubai. When asked about the secret of his success, Ravi said, 'Have the courage to dream. Follow your dreams, believe in them; your passion and performance will propel them to become a reality.'

Behind the Scenes

Ravi's real-life success story is an excellent example of sheer grit, determination and self-belief. Ravi had a rough road to success. However, he saw multiple possibilities in the field of construction and did not shy away from taking risks and facing failures. His passion for work, self-confidence and desire to excel ignited his zeal to create and take on new opportunities.

When people are unsure of themselves, they become afraid to take necessary risks, which can further make them inflexible. Excessive reliance on others for validation could cause people around them to become irritated and ultimately alienate them. The basic difficulty in becoming self-reliant is overcoming emotional dependency and feelings of insecurity while building confidence. Human fears such as those of failure, being judged or being alienated often are also at the core of insecurities.

Ravi is a true business leader icon and scores very highly on the emotional intelligence scale. He demonstrates the ability to be independent in his thinking and actions. A healthy sense of self-reliance is necessary in today's business world. Self-reliance arises from a deep trust in our strength to face our responsibilities head on and overcome patterns of dependency that have controlled our performance in the past. Plato said that every human being is fighting the battle between the two parts of themselves—the child and the adult. The child remains controlled by fear and insecurity and wants to remain dependant on other adults. The adult wants to overcome fears and act freely and creatively. So at each moment, we choose whether to allow the child or the adult to determine our thoughts and actions.

In addition to strengthening leadership presence, building emotional self-reliance frees up a lot of creative energy. As self-confidence builds, so does trust—and so do innovative ideas coupled with the capacity to take risks. This is the expected pay-off of becoming more independent.

TOOLBOX   Develop Self-reliance

Self-reliance refers to the ability to function autonomously and rests on one's degree of self-confidence, inner strength and desire to take crucial decisions and meet obligations. The tool below will help you to take independent decisions.

Please read the following instructions:

- Visualise yourself taking a crucial decision. What are the implications of your decision?
- Visualise the situation post the implementation of your decision. Note it down and share it with everyone.

Sometimes, decisions may be difficult. For example, in a situation where you have a star performer who is also a troublemaker. How will you handle the situation? Can you visualise such real-life situations?

Know More: What Differentiates Great Leaders from Everyone Else?

In his book *Emotional Capitalists*, Martyn Newman summarised the research on the personal qualities of successful leaders.

- Successful leaders score high on self-reliance, assertiveness (self-expression) and optimism. These three competencies enable leaders to model self-assured behaviour, communicate a clear view of the organisation's vision and direction, inspire the confidence of others and deal with setbacks in a positive and constructive way.
- Self-reliance is the most important signature strength for creating emotional capital. It involves two emotional competencies: self-reliance—the

(Continued)

(Continued)

recognition that each of us is a complete and self-directed individual and has the ability to make decisions, and self-belief—the ability to have confidence in our judgement and the readiness to take action to achieve our goals.

- A leader's emotional desire to remain dependant and escape from responsibility can lead to paralysis in decision-making or to acting impulsively—both techniques to avoid responsible, thoughtful choices. To emerge from this paralysis, we must shift focus from pleasing others and worrying about their potential judgements to trusting our own views and communicating them clearly. A straightforward and respectful manner of communication demonstrates responsibility for our own views and behaviour and enables us to allow others to do the same; in other words, 'have little interest in proving ourselves, but a continuous interest in expressing ourselves'.

SCENE 4

Going with the Flow

VINOD'S STORY: GOING WITH THE FLOW ... AND THEN DIRECTING IT

One day, Vinod came home and broke the news to his wife and his son, Harsh, that he had been transferred to Pune. But he did not tell them the whole story.

Vinod was a quiet worker, always believing that the quality of his work would speak for itself. Unfortunately, his peers took advantage of his silence and shamelessly took credit for Vinod's work. Vinod's old boss had recently left the company, and the new boss did not bother to validate the team members' claims. Instead, he put greater pressure on Vinod to improve his performance.

Subsequently, at the area strategy meet, it was decided that only the top performing members would remain in Mumbai. With Vinod unwilling to market himself, the senior leaders were unable to see any tangible results from Vinod's contribution, so the boss transferred him to the Pune office. Vinod was less than happy about the change. He felt bitter that his work had not been recognised and that he was now being dumped into the Pune office.

Harsh, Vinod's son, was 15 at the time and about to take the Class X board exams. Not wanting to disrupt Harsh's education, Vinod decided that he alone would move to Pune, visiting his wife and son on weekends.

Work life in Pune was not the same as in Mumbai. Vinod tried to alter his work habits, but after 20 years, it was difficult for him to change the way he worked. The nature of the work was different and the people he was working with were more relaxed. There was no sense of urgency or drive for excellence, such as in the Mumbai office. Vinod was irritated by this new work culture and often felt very frustrated. He lost interest in his work.

> Vinod is flustered and annoyed by his new environment. An important aspect of adaptability is the power to be flexible and take different perspectives into account. It affects our overall ability to adapt to new, unfamiliar and unpredictable circumstances. In the rapidly changing world in which we live, adaptability gains prominence. It enables us to be comfortable with ambiguity and to remain calm in the face of the unexpected.

Within a few months of the move, Vinod was called to Mumbai for an urgent meeting with his boss. The boss had noticed that Vinod was finding it difficult to adjust to the new environment. He could not get along with his team in Pune and had also not performed satisfactorily. The management thought it best to part ways now, while it could still be done amicably. Vinod's biggest fear turned to reality when he was asked to sign a voluntary retirement scheme. He walked out of the room in a daze.

Vinod had held the same job for the last two decades. It was such an integral part of his being that he simply could not reconcile to the fact that he had been forced to quit and that he would now have to work in an entirely new set-up.

What would you do differently if you were in Vinod's situation? In what ways has he become his own biggest obstacle?

Vinod spent a few weeks at home and coached Harsh for his exams. Thankfully, Harsh aced his papers, especially English. He was able to get into a junior college and a course of his choice.

After a while, Vinod's wife gently suggested that Vinod begin looking for a job. Reluctantly, Vinod dragged himself to the computer and decided to update his curriculum vitae (CV), after 20 years of being in a stable job. He began sending out job applications in response to vacancy ads in the newspaper and online portals. Over the next few months, Vinod was on the receiving end of a series of rejections. When his wife offered to call her friend's husband for advice, Vinod refused, saying that was not how he wanted to approach this problem. He was also unwilling to contact former colleagues who were now in other companies for information on current openings that would be relevant to his experience.

And so the half-hearted job hunt went on, month after month. Finally, Vinod decided to give up the search and spend his time coaching children for their school exams. He would spend a couple of hours every day tutoring children from the neighbourhood.

People who are high on adaptability are able to handle transitions smoothly and work with multiple demands. They are open to different viewpoints and are willing to change their approach in favour of a more effective one. They are likely to take risks and begin new projects. They are able to change before the external push appears, that is, before it is too late. Pay special attention to the different ways in which Vinod and Harsh handle change.

Meanwhile, his father's experience made Harsh grow up suddenly. In his third year of college, he felt the need to stand on his own feet and take responsibility for himself. He did not want to be a burden on his parents any longer. Harsh had always wanted to be a lawyer, but it proved next to impossible to find a paid internship in the field. Harsh's friend recommended he take up an opening at an upcoming magazine, and so Harsh decided to put his writing skills to the test and began freelancing for the magazine.

Having always aspired to be a lawyer, Harsh had never noticed that he had a flair for writing. Upon graduating, he decided to give writing a fair chance and joined the magazine full-time. Within a few months, he realised that this was something he could see himself doing for the rest of his life. Harsh used his savings from the magazine job and obtained a scholarship to fund himself through the Master's course in journalism at the University of London.

Harsh, now a promising 25-year-old journalist, often thinks back to the summer of 2005. He reminisces about what the family and especially his father went through at that time. He realised that this situation had taught him so much—most of all, that every situation throws up opportunities. It is up to us to recognise these opportunities and act upon them. If it was not for his father's experiences, he may have never discovered his true calling. It is no surprise that Harsh's favourite saying is 'There truly is a silver lining on every grey cloud.'

Behind the Scenes

Adaptability is the ability to adjust our emotions, thoughts and behaviour to changing situations and conditions and to remain open to change, new ideas, challenges and approaches. These skills are integral to survival and growth.

The key to adaptability is to learn to change before we are forced to, before it is too late. Let us look at Vinod's life. Vinod was unhappy when he was asked to move to Pune. Yet, he did nothing to remedy the situation. Even after he was fired, Vinod did not know how to deal with the situation and wasted a lot of time before looking for a new job. While job-hunting, he took his time to respond to ads and vacancies. Despite the fact that newspapers and online job postings were not yielding results, Vinod did not think of changing his strategy, nor was he keen on turning to his family and friends for help.

His son, Harsh, however, showed high levels of adaptability. He was able to keep pace with the big changes at home and still manage to get good grades. When he realised there was a financial crunch at home, he stepped up to the occasion and began working. He was flexible in his choice of work—despite having a leaning towards law, he willingly took up a writing job. Having given it an honest try, Harsh discovered that he really was good at writing and finally went on to make a career of it. Unlike his father, he made the best of a bad situation and found a new path to follow. As it turned out, he discovered that this path was his true calling.

In today's competitive and dynamic world, with market conditions changing in the blink of an eye, leaders are required to make quick changes and to develop new strategies in line with ever-changing demands and trends. In order to do this, leaders need to conquer the fear of the unknown and learn to be comfortable with a certain degree of uncertainty. Adaptability is the basis of important leadership competencies such as problem-solving, conflict resolution and negotiation.

As we see from Vinod's and Harsh's stories, adaptability not only ensures success but also creates leaders who shape their dreams using the resources available to them at any given time.

TOOLBOX   Action Plan for a More Flexible You

Steps		What are you going to do?
1	Write down your personal fears related to the change you are going through. Who could you talk to about them?	
2	What would you like to learn about the change? Who can provide you with the information?	
3	Imagine an image of the future, to which the change is supposed to lead. What actions will you take?	
4	Who can help you to enter your new role? Who can help you to test new solutions?	
5	What did the experience of change teach you? If you experience another change in the future, what could you do better?	

Navigating Daily Obstacles

Problem-solving

'Difficulties in your life do not come to destroy you, but to help you realise your hidden potential and power. Let difficulties know that you too are difficult.'

~ A.P.J. Abdul Kalam

SANDEEP'S STORY: TRIPPING UP ON HURDLES

As Sandeep rushed into his office on the morning of Friday, 23 December, he thought of all that had to be done at work that day before his long-awaited weekend getaway would begin. When his friends planned a short but promising holiday over the Christmas weekend at a farmhouse in Lonavla, he had jumped at the opportunity. He desperately needed a break after all the late nights and weekends that he had spent at work lately.

Recently, Sandeep's zonal manager, Mr Rathore, had put him in charge of a new, prestigious strategic initiative at the bank to reduce the time taken to convert a lead into an account. The plan was to identify non-value-adding activities and streamline the process to make it more hassle-free for customers, so there would be fewer opportunities for them to be lured away by other banks. Sandeep had the opportunity to work with a cross-vertical team to make this happen. The first step was to collect information around customer

acquisition, customer complaints and other recommendations from across the organisation. Sandeep would then plot
the process steps that each customer went through and identify the customers' pain points. On the basis of this analysis,
a new process would be created that would be implemented
across the organisation.

Sandeep outlined a plan for completing the project within
three months. Today's task was a first-level analysis of customer complaint data that he was to receive from three different departments across the bank. Sandeep had been
promised some information on the basis of which he was to
complete the first-level analysis. Since this was the first time
he was doing such a project, he was not sure how long it
would take, but estimated it could be completed in about
four hours. The team would definitely have something ready
before they broke for Christmas weekend. He could also ask
his manager for help if need be.

> Problem-solving is a basic prerequisite for making decisions, especially
> strategic planning. Note that Sandeep has not gathered enough infor-
> mation about the scope and timelines of a project that is unfamiliar to
> him. Should he have consulted his manager to get a project overview
> before making his assessment?

No sooner had Sandeep seated himself in his office, he
was called in to a meeting to discuss the sales figures. At the
end of the meeting, Mr Rathore enquired about the project
status. Sandeep happily responded that he was waiting for
the data to come in and would work on it soon after. Pleased,
Mr Rathore decided he would deliver the first-level analysis
presentation to his seniors on Monday. Sandeep nodded his
head, glad that he had a chance to prove his worth to Mr
Rathore.

On his way back to his workstation, Sandeep got a call
about a customer who required his immediate attention.
While rushing to the first floor, he heard a ping on his

Blackberry. He smiled as he saw that the first batch of data had come in. He rushed to the branch manager's office to sort out the irate customer's problem. He was listening patiently to the customer when the phone buzzed—another set of data points were in his inbox. Now all he needed was the data from the corporate accounts vertical.

From the manager's office, Sandeep rushed straight back to his station. He wondered whether he should start work on next week's presentation or wait for the last piece of data. He called corporate accounts, who said they had some critical work at the moment but would send the data soon. Sandeep looked at his watch—his friends were expected to pick him up in an hour's time! He decided there was nothing to do but send one last reminder to corporate accounts to send in the data by the weekend. He would work on it first thing Monday morning. There was no point working on the analysis in a piecemeal manner. Besides, right now his head was brimming with thoughts of his much anticipated Christmas weekend.

> People who are good at problem-solving are able to anticipate and deal with potentially complex problems. When Sandeep does not receive all the information he needs, he fails to see the larger picture and antici-pate that this may create an obstacle. He makes a quick call and sends a brief email instead of creating a sense of urgency with the other team about the presentation on Monday. Furthermore, Sandeep does not keep his superiors in the loop about the possible delay.

On the morning of 24 December, Sandeep sleepily answered his phone in Lonavla. The person on the other end sounded frantic. It took him a minute to realise that it was Mr Rathore enquiring about the first-level analysis. Sandeep immediately sat up straight and quickly answered that he had not received all the data in time and that he was pre-pared to work on it as soon as he got it. When asked what he was doing about it, he was silent. Mr Rathore explained that he had to present the analysis to his seniors at 2 p.m. on Monday so he would need it in his inbox latest by noon. Sandeep promised that it would get done. Yet, as he put the phone down, he felt uncomfortable and anxious. How was he going to manage this? He thought of calling someone for help, but he did not want to share credit on such a critical project. After all, this was his one chance to prove his worth directly to the zonal manager.

Sandeep decided he would go in early on Monday (26 December) and complete the work. It would take him an hour to arrange the data, another hour to analyse it and then an hour to quickly document the analysis. So if he reached office at 8.30 a.m., he could easily have the presentation ready by 11.30 a.m., giving him half an hour of buffer time. 'Yes, that will work,' he thought.

> Sandeep promises to deliver the data in time; yet, he does not exert himself to proactively find an effective solution. Instead, he presumes the best-case scenario and ends up with an illogical solution that has the potential to cause more problems. People with poor problem-solving abilities often make hasty, ill-thought-out decisions or avoid making a decision altogether.

On Monday, Sandeep woke up early, but got stuck in a traffic jam, only reaching office by 9.30 a.m. 'No need to worry, still plenty of time,' he thought. When he checked his inbox, he realised that the last batch of data had still not come in. That is when Sandeep started to panic. He called Corporate Accounts hysterically. It took them a while to locate the concerned person and finally get him on the line. Sandeep screamed at him, asking for the information—*right this minute.*

It was now 10.15 a.m. Sandeep opened the two sets of data he had received on Friday and realised that one of the sheets had a lot of extraneous data. It took him a substantial amount of time to extract the information he needed. Why hadn't he checked the file and done this on Friday? He could have saved so much time! Sandeep thought of calling his manager, but decided to use those precious minutes to work instead. Moreover, he was now scared that he would be under fire for leaving things to the last minute if he went to the manager.

As the clock struck 12, Sandeep was not even halfway done. With his heart in his throat, he continued to type away furiously. He was so tense he could barely process the data he was reading. As he knew it would, the phone began to ring insistently; Mr Rathore was on the line.

Behind the Scenes

Sandeep is good at his work but lacks problem-solving skills—the ability to identify and solve daily problems. Problem-solving includes weighing the pros and cons of various potential solutions and foreseeing their possible outcomes. Sandeep repeatedly failed to consider multiple options and anticipate the results of his actions (or the lack thereof). When things did not go according to plan, he panicked and fell apart.

Problem-solving is an asset to a leader as well as the organisation as it allows both to adapt to a dynamic environment as well as to tide over crises. Inherent in problem-solving is the ability to cope with problematic situations in order to improve them. This is an important skill for individual contributors and senior leaders. It is especially useful for judges, production planning managers, airplane pilots and engineers, as these professions use this skill on a daily basis.

People who lack problem-solving skills tend to get stuck when faced with a problem, such as Sandeep. They may be unable to generate many solutions or unable to see a problem from different perspectives. They may have difficulty in seeing the causal relationship between an event and its effect. They may also find it tough to anticipate difficulties. For instance, when the last set of data was delayed, Sandeep did not think and plan ahead. He could have checked that the two data sets that were already with him were correctly formatted and done at least a preliminary analysis on Friday itself. Sandeep was also unwilling to ask for help as this means he may have to share the glory. Perhaps a better way to approach the issue would be to ensure a successful outcome first, and then consider who gets the credit for it.

People with strong problem-solving abilities tend to approach problems head-on and proactively solve them. They try to collect as much information as possible; based on this, they make good decisions. They can quickly identify problems and push forward to overcome them.

TOOLBOX   Problem-solving

Is there a current problem I am procrastinating on?

What kind of problems do I tend to avoid? (Think of three recent examples where you have ignored problems and they have blown up into larger issues.)

Why do I avoid these problems? What holds me back from addressing these problems?

How can I overcome this reluctance to solve problems? (A few options are given below.)

- Change the self-talk to make problems seem like exciting challenges
- Reach out to someone for help—to make you be aware of occasions when you are effective and when you are less effective in your problem-solving

- Think of ways to anticipate problems
- Think of why it is critical for you to deal with the problem
- Reflect on the consequences of not dealing with the issue immediately
- Reflect on times when you have dealt with problems in a timely manner

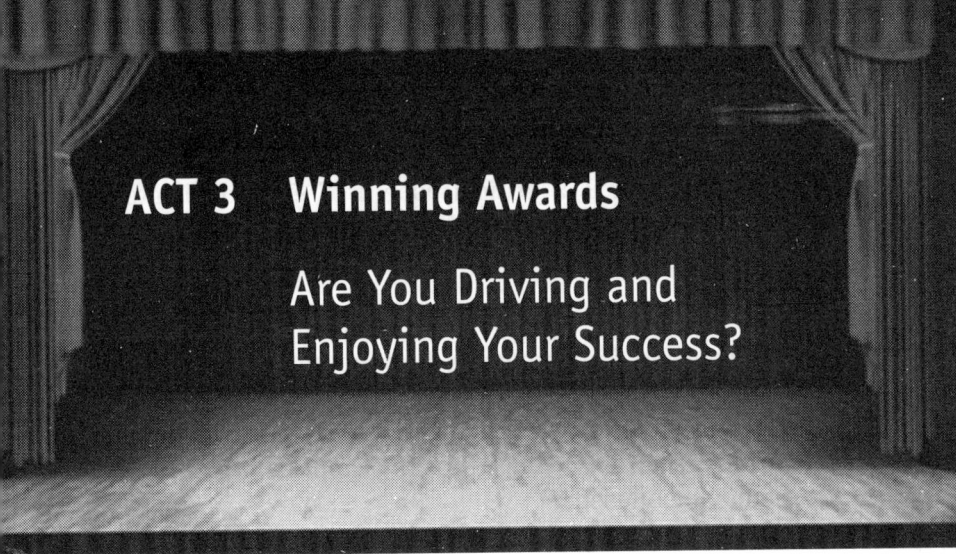

ACT 3 Winning Awards

Are You Driving and Enjoying Your Success?

Self-motivation

'Our way of thinking creates good or bad outcomes.'

~ Stephen Richards

INTRODUCTION TO SELF-MOTIVATION

Wouldn't it be great if we all had a personal cheerleader or coach to lift our spirits and keep us going when we felt overcome by challenges or found our enthusiasm waning? Many times, other people in our lives do take on the role of a motivator—parents, friends, colleagues, bosses and so on. But the most important wellspring of motivation lies *within* each of us. We are best equipped to identify our own 'low' phases—periods when we battle pessimism, procrastination and negativity. At times like this, we become our own worst enemy, standing in the way of our cherished dreams.

Once you develop the capability to rouse yourself out of this state and get back on the path to your goal, there is no limit to what you can achieve at work—and in life. Inspiration, creativity and productivity flourish when you are in a positive state of mind and focused on your objectives.

Self-motivation is a critical aspect of emotional intelligence. Quite simply, self-motivation means the ability to motivate oneself. The three qualities that comprise self-motivation are:

- *Optimism*: Expecting the best outcome, even in the face of adversity.
- *Achievement drive*: Striving to realise one's potential.
- *Contentment*: Having a positive approach to life and enjoying oneself.

In this section, you will find a series of stories that illustrate these three qualities. At various points in the stories, you will be given an insight into how these individuals use the power of self-motivation to transform their dreams into reality. These stories will be followed by exercises that help you tangibly apply the concept of self-motivation to your particular experiences and situation.

SCENE 1

Staying Away from the Dark Side

Optimism

'Optimism is the faith that leads to achievement. Nothing can be done without hope and confidence.'

~ Helen Keller

AFZAL'S STORY: HOLDING ON TO POSITIVITY AND PASSION

Succumbing to the pressure from his father, a professor of engineering, Afzal agreed to take up engineering as a career. While Afzal did have a scientific bent of mind, his true calling lay elsewhere—in the world of design and fine arts. When he voiced his desire to enter the world of art at age 15, Afzal's father was not very happy. He explained that making it big in the world of art would be difficult. After all, art was not really the most lucrative of careers and Afzal had to earn a living eventually. Afzal understood his father's viewpoint, but his heart was not in engineering.

He grudgingly went through college, learning subjects that he was not interested in, just about scraping through the exams—all because he believed there was no option. At one point, after seeing his performance, his father asked him to reconsider his career path. However, having struggled through four years of engineering college, Afzal did not see the point in making a change now and so he continued to trudge onwards.

> Optimists look at the brighter side of life and maintain a positive attitude even in the face of adversity. Pessimists, however, tend to give up more easily. Afzal is sure he will not like engineering but is not motivated enough to speak to his father about an alternative career. Instead, he passively accepts his father's decision.

Fresh out of college, Afzal was recruited by Promote, a leading MNC in the space of IT. Within his first few weeks in the organisation, Afzal was sent to their head office in Paris for six months of induction.

On his return from France, his supervisor, Mr Janardhan, found that Afzal was not performing up to the mark. He did not like following processes; he neglected developmental inputs; but most worrying of all were his low energy levels. Mr Janardhan could not imagine why a young man was so demotivated at the very beginning of his career. He felt that Afzal lacked the drive and willingness to learn—qualities that were most valued in new recruits. He examined Afzal's earlier performance in Promote. His trainer testified that he had a sharp mind but gave up easily; conversations with his peers revealed that he was a bright and valuable resource but did not exert himself when the task was not to his liking. He was a pleasant person, but was not showing results.

Mr Janardhan saw a spark in Afzal and decided to take him under his wing. He called Afzal into his office and informed him that for the next three months they would be working closely on the development of a new app. The project would require not just technical expertise but also the ability to plan well and to liaise with various content writers and design experts. This was a new venture for the company, and he hoped it would prove exciting for Afzal.

Afzal, however, was terrified. He could see that he was taken off the old project because of his incompetence and that the new project required a lot of work. He would certainly have to stretch beyond office timings to complete his task. The complex nature of the task made him feel like he was being set up for failure. All kinds of fears flooded Afzal's mind. He decided to ask Mr Janardhan to get one more person on the project to support him. There was no way he could do this on his own.

> Afzal gives in to his apprehensions and sees Mr Janardhan's efforts as a punishment. Even before the project begins, he is convinced that he will not be able to handle it well.

Mr Janardhan, however, politely refused to add another person to the team. He felt Afzal was capable and the project was just starting out. They could get support later if necessary.

At first, Afzal was dejected and often felt like giving up. But there was a mountain of work to be done and he did not have time to brood. Mr Janardhan constantly pushed him, providing support wherever required.

However, when Afzal began working with the design team, his joy was evident. He looked forward to the meetings with them. They too found it easy to communicate with him, as he was aesthetically inclined and his ideas were novel. Mr Janardhan realised that Afzal's performance was peaking, perhaps because he was working around an area of interest—designing. Gradually building his confidence by giving him stretch goals around designing the app and also supporting him in areas where he was not good, Mr Janardhan helped Afzal create a great product. Afzal realised that he had found his niche.

> Pay special note to how Afzal's supervisor, Mr Janardhan, chooses the path of optimism. He believes in Afzal's potential and is keen to give him a chance. He actively coaches Afzal through the project, helping him play to his strengths.

At the end of the project, Mr Janardhan had a review with Afzal. He asked him to list out the differences in the two projects that he had worked on, including the difference in his attitude towards the two. That is where it became clear—the distinction between his 'I'm doing this because I have to do this, there's no point in giving my best' attitude in the first project and the 'I enjoy doing this and I must do it well' attitude in the second project.

Afzal realised that while it was important to pursue his strengths, right through his life he had always given up when faced with adversities rather than manage them with optimism and hope. Faced with roadblocks, whether from his father at the time of choosing his career or even now when he was allocated maintenance projects that required a high degree of process follow-up, he simply gave up. He usually heard an 'inner voice' that told him—*it won't work, there's no point.*

But now, after his first taste of success, he was willing to change and challenge that pessimistic inner voice whenever it tried to pull him down.

Behind the Scenes

In this real-life story of Afzal, we see how a lack of optimism can make all the difference between a mediocre career and a success story. In the beginning, Afzal was repeatedly defeated by his negative outlook. Had he adopted a positive outlook and believed in himself, he might have been able to convince his father about his true calling. Even if he decided to compromise and pursue engineering anyway, he would have put in more effort to overcome the challenges.

Optimism plays a vital role in overall self-motivation and is a very important factor in reaching goals and coping with stress. All of us experience the same life events, but optimists are more likely to get through these situations and bounce back quickly from defeat because they look at their mistakes as learning experiences.

People who are optimistic have the drive and motivation to succeed in their work and in their private life. This enables them to keep trying despite setbacks, until they eventually succeed. Giving in to negative emotions can pull people down, making it difficult to establish meaningful interpersonal relationships at work as well as in personal life. It compromises effective interaction and performance in teams and organisations.

Staying upbeat is thus a crucial element in dealing with the change, uncertainty and entrepreneurial risk that is all too prevalent in today's dynamic environment. It keeps you going and helps you tide over difficult times—coming out stronger on the other side!

Know More: Dadasaheb Phalke—Impossible Is Nothing

The story of Dadasaheb Phalke, the father of the Indian film industry, is a shining, real-life example of the power of a positive attitude. His story underscores the importance of infectious enthusiasm and enduring belief in one's goal.

In 1913, after a fallout with a business partner, Dadasaheb Phalke decided to make his own silent motion picture. He made several attempts but success eluded him. He finally realised that he needed to learn new film-making methods that were available only in England.

Around this time, his wife was pregnant with their third child, so his friends tried to dissuade him from going to England and attend to his family instead. However, Phalke had faith that things would eventually turn out well; his family supported his decision, too. He sold all his worldly possessions, purchased a ticket and—without a contact or a place to stay—set sail for

(Continued)

(Continued)

London. His optimistic attitude paid off when he found the training course he was looking for; luckily, he made friends with a Maharashtrian restaurateur who provided him with food and shelter.

Phalke did not waste time thinking of the obstacles that could crop up in his way. He spent night after night at the theatre, keenly observing the techniques used. He even temporarily lost his eyesight due to exertion! Everyone thought him crazy, but Phalke was driven by a big dream—establishing a film industry in India. He garnered support from all sources possible.

When Phalke returned to India, he insisted that his wife learn the technical aspects of film-making (mixing chemicals, processing prints, etc.) and, contrary to the tradition at the time, contemplated asking women to play the female roles in his first movie. He even visited a red-light district in his quest to find female actors.

Phalke was able to bring together a team of actors and technicians to produce his first film—the story of King Harishchandra. Thanks to his passion and hard work, the movie became a hit and marked the beginning of one of the world's biggest film industries.

Phalke was positive and relentless in the pursuit of his dream. He worked tirelessly to get people interested in films, dispelling the myths that surrounded cinema. (One such far-fetched misconception was that clicking a photo sucked the life out of the subject!)

Phalke left no stone unturned to bring people to the theatre. His innovative advertising attracted not only Indians but also the Britishers in India. In fact, the British actively supported him.

As a result of his upbeat approach and boundless enthusiasm, Dadasaheb Phalke achieved his seemingly impossible goal. Today, he is revered as the founder of the Indian film industry.

TOOLBOX   Overcoming Negativity

Identify a current situation in which you are feeling stuck:

- Write down all the reasons why this should work in your favour.
- Write down the feelings you are experiencing.
- Write down the roadblocks you need to overcome.
- Commit to action.

SCENE 2

Striving to Realise Your Potential

Achievement Drive

'We must always strive for excellence. But excellence cannot be imposed from the outside. We must feel the need from within. It must become an obsession. It must involve not only our mind but our heart and soul. Excellence is not an act but a habit... ultimately, your only competition is yourself.'

~ Azim Premji

PETER'S STORY: KNOWING WHAT YOU WANT AND GOING FOR IT!

Peter had been born with a silver spoon in his mouth. His father, Sylvester Lobo, was the CEO of one of the fastest-growing telecom handset manufacturers in the country. Sylvester was a simple man with a humble education. However, he had the passion to turn things around. His dream was to free the Indian economy from its dependence on foreign brands. Given the growth of the telecom sector, Sylvester smartly laid all his bets on handset manufacturing. He made a small start, but the promise of the industry was not lost on him. Over the next 20 years, his company Georgius had multiplied its revenue many times over. At the end of his stint as the CEO, he could only hope his sons would do as much justice to his brainchild as he had once dreamt of.

A critical factor in personal success, such as Sylvester Lobo's, is the ability to know what you want, to have a sense of direction in life and to strive to realise your potential. Achievement drive manifests itself in our involvement in pursuits that lead to a meaningful life. It is an ongoing, dynamic process of striving towards maximum development of our abilities, capabilities and talents.

Sylvester's sons, Peter and Christopher, were as different as chalk and cheese. Christopher, his older son, was mature and always stuck to the rule book. He was also extremely hard-working and diligent, much like his father. He would hardly ever venture into the unknown, but had the will to excel at whatever was delegated to him. Peter, however, was daring and never afraid to experiment with something new. Wild though he was sometimes, he was focused; once he set a goal for himself, all he could see was the eye of the fish.

Sylvester had ensured that his sons were inducted into the company at junior management levels so they could understand and appreciate the nuances of the business. Over the last few years, they had both done exceptionally well in certain areas and proved themselves across projects. Sylvester had no qualms in handing over the reins now; he had taught them well.

Christopher stuck to the traditional path and diligently followed what his father had started. He made a good manager who would stay focused on the task at hand and deliver the expected results. He considered the work force in Georgius the most important asset and ensured that they felt valued. It was one big family—people were comfortable in their jobs and had been a part of the organisation for years. Peter, however, was raring to go. He was always talking about his plans for expansion, greater market coverage and deriving higher productivity from the same assets. He dreamt of taking the business overseas. This dream provided a thrill and fuelled the drive in him, and the need to feel this thrill brought about razor-sharp focus. Peter could not imagine living his life in a comfort zone and easy stretch. The excitement and internal high of achieving goals defined life for him.

Despite several attempts, it seemed to Peter that Chris's aversion to risks was binding him down to the usual way of doing business. Chris needed to conform. Because it was important for him to do the right thing by everybody—risking anything for their future was inconceivable. In contrast, Peter felt his big dream would take care of the entire team's future, so where was the risk?

> Note the attributes of diligence, passion and focus exhibited by both Peter and Christopher. However, 'drive' is what separates the two. The need and drive to achieve is one of the strongest factors that distinguishes high performers from average performers. Whether for an individual or an organisation, achievement drive represents a sense of direction, purpose and meaning. It is this that leads to a sense of fulfilment beyond materialistic measures of success.

In the various discussions that took place, Peter asked and later demanded to be given responsibility for sales of a demarcated geographic region. He was confident, to the point of being arrogant, that he could make a high profit. He was grudgingly handed a South India region that was considered a high-cost structure due to the low productivity that the region offered. The company was planning to shut down the non-profitable unit, and Peter was given the opportunity to make one last attempt at managing the Chennai office, although people more senior and skilled than him had tried earlier—and failed.

Peter's first day in office was a day of significant distress for him and the staff. The South India region, with all of 300 employees, was in complete disarray as compared to the head office. Punctuality and professionalism were almost non-existent in the Chennai office, and Peter found himself doubting the corporate HR's capability to monitor the locations. People in this office, it seemed, had grown resistant to change; they did not appreciate the intrusion of the young progeny from the corporate office. Peter observed a growing sense of complacency amongst the people and also some amount of bitterness towards the corporate office. The bar of excellence had fallen very low so even shoddy work was acceptable.

However, Peter was undeterred; he thrived on challenges and knew exactly what he wanted: Georgius was to set sail for larger territories and invade bigger markets. His immediate goal was to double the current profitability of the Chennai office and to give it a reason to not shut down—and he had more than one way of getting there. The first and foremost measure was to stop being a non-resident regional manager; therefore, against the wishes of his loving family, he moved to the unknown city.

From the first moment in office, Peter was always racing against time; he brought a strange fervour into the place that the employees in Chennai had never known. With the boss always in office, employees were forced to reach on time and put in late hours. They all detested it.

Over the years, Georgius had increasingly become an inward-looking organisation with little idea about outside competition. With the help of past data, Peter soon realised that they were losing a number of deals to competition. He wasted no time in setting up a cross-functional team within the organisation to study market dynamics and consumer demands and to understand what their competitors were doing better. After three days (and nights) of intense research, the team presented their findings along with possible suggestions. Peter had all workable recommendations actioned immediately.

> Peter is undeterred by challenges because he is clear about his big-picture goal, and about his ability to ensure his company gets there. Achievement-oriented individuals set themselves challenging yet realistic goals; in their pursuit of those goals, they are ready to take calculated risks. Highly achievement-oriented individuals believe in doing every task they take up to the best of their ability.

Peter also took some extreme measures, armed with his motto of 'what's worth doing is worth doing well'. He used frequent reviews to understand the ground reality of his reportees, which made senior members of his team uncomfortable. They were not used to anything other than an occasional review in a five-star hotel. During most of these meetings, Peter engaged in solving one problem or another and was known for pushing his team members out of their comfort zones. While most dreaded the reviews, the few who were more ambitious began to look up to him. Peter brought with him some very good practices none of them had heard of before. They were told to place a strategic intent behind every action they took—everything they did must somehow lead to the commitment made at the beginning of the year. Peter never hesitated to take a call, even late at night, from any of his people or to accompany them for closures on big deals. For the first time in years, it seemed as if the Chennai office had breathed some life into itself. The employees felt they had the tools to succeed.

> Individuals high on achievement drive persistently strive to do their best, constantly working on self-improvement in general, which in turn leads to feelings of self-satisfaction. They usually have a good idea of how they want their lives to play out and always try to find a sense of meaning in what they do. They are highly goal oriented and consistent in their drive to meet their objectives and standards. Pay special note to how Peter's drive for excellence inspires some of his team members—infusing them with the passion to succeed as well.

Georgius soon acquired and successfully closed their first big lead. Peter gave all the credit to his team and threw a lavish lunch party. After all, the Chennai region had hit their first home run. By and by, other wins came their way, and the team began to rejoice in the wake of these successes. They hungered for more, and the team geared up to do better. They no longer harboured a grudge against hard work, now that they had had a taste of success. Soon, their growing performance had the corporate office taking notice of them. Peter was fast becoming a figure of respect. His people turned to him when in need of direction or looking for solutions to complex problems.

Within a year and a half, the Chennai region had begun meeting its monthly revenue targets; they were known throughout the country for their seemingly unconventional way of doing business, in that they did everything in their power to close deals. Their region also boasted of having the most productive workforce pan India. Yes, they were not following rules and processes to the hilt, but they were showing results. Things were looking up under the leadership of the young prodigy whom people had once refused to take seriously.

After two years of rigorous hard work, and under Peter's leadership, the South India region soon opened their first office in Colombo. It was a moment of great joy and immense pride for the entire family, Christopher included.

Behind the Scenes

The above story highlights Peter's high achievement drive, characterised by his need to excel. While Peter was experimental and occasionally wild in his youth, he grew up to become a confident and focused person. From a young age, he spoke of plans for expansion, greater market coverage and deriving higher productivity. He knew what he needed to succeed and asked for control of one location. When he was handed a failing location, he was not disheartened. Instead, he saw it as an opportunity. This optimistic attitude fuelled by his natural thirst for challenge and internal drive helped him focus on the overall objective of increasing sales.

Peter learned to use unconventional means to achieve results. Driven by his passion and under his leadership, the team too began to perform well. Peter kept his eye on the goal; his frequent review meetings strengthened the focus on the sales figures the team needed to achieve. Peter's determination to do well made him examine the cause of their past failure and look at industry information to improve current practices. He engaged in problem-solving with the team to get past hurdles. Their first taste of success made the whole team keen to work harder. And it was ultimately Peter's passion and excitement that translated into accolades for the whole team.

Conversely, low achievement drive in an individual implies a lack of direction or purpose, lack of a dream and lack of vision, often associated with a sense of emptiness. Individuals or organisations with low levels of achievement drive are not able to set challenging goals, are happy enough to maintain the status quo and are more than willing to pursue simple goals without a sense of purpose.

Some people may not know what they want to achieve because they are confused about themselves and what they want to do in life. Others may know what they want to accomplish but are unable to realise their potential. These situations could lead to feelings of frustration or depression, resulting in withdrawal from interests, lack of drive for improvement, a feeling of general helplessness and dissatisfaction with life.

We can improve our achievement drive by taking a few simple steps such as setting realistic yet challenging goals for ourselves at work and in our personal lives. We then need to make a genuine effort to reach those goals and reward ourselves each time we accomplish a goal. Even small efforts such as completing any task that we have started and not postponing important tasks until the last minute are actions that could lead to success in building our achievement drive. The ultimate objective would be to realise our potential and the value of what we do, and to use this to motivate ourselves to greater heights in life.

TOOLBOX   Achievement Drive

This exercise will help you establish and focus on your aspirations.

A big part of having a strong achievement drive is knowing what you want to achieve. The following is a goal-setting exercise designed to help you become clearer on your small and big picture.

Please list three personal and professional goals for the following:

a. For today
b. For this month
c. For this year
d. For the next five years

Imagine a date 5 years from now—imagine your life at that time.	
Imagine what a typical day would be like.	
What would you be doing—work life and personal life?	
Who would be around you?	
What would be your thoughts and feelings?	

Now create a 'bucket list'. What are the goals or dreams you want to achieve before you die? For example, improve writing skills, learn to dance, become senior manager, found your own company, travel the world and so on. Dream big—write the list as though there is no chance for failure (but keep it realistic to your particular strengths and circumstances).

SCENE 3

Having a Positive Approach to Life and Enjoying Yourself

Contentment

'I hope you achieve success in whatever way you define it and what gives you the maximum happiness in life.'

~ Azim Premji

RADHA'S STORY: THE GLASS IS ALWAYS HALF FULL FOR WINNERS

'Your EI scores in empathy and in interpersonal relations seem to be good,' said the consultant. Radha's eyes wandered to the tool and widened in surprise—she was shocked at her low score in contentment. 'But ...' she said, 'I can't understand this. I mean, I'm doing well. I got that promotion two months back and I'm really happy about it—so obviously I'm content.'

Radha, a pleasant lady with about 10 years of experience, was getting feedback on the Personal EQ Meter, an EI assessment tool. Her consultant discovered she was not willing to believe her low contentment score, so he decided to explore it further and said, 'Tell me about the time when you were happiest.'

It did not take long for Radha to say that it was during her school days. Radha had been a fun-loving girl, involved in a number of extra-curricular activities, while doing well at her studies at the same time. Both her parents and her teachers acknowledged her efforts and talent. She remembered this phase of her life, wistfully, as being the happiest—she felt she could touch the skies. As she recalled those days, the consultant often noticed her eyes sparkle and her face light up with joy.

Contentment is the ability to enjoy ourselves, others and life in general. It stems from self-satisfaction, is associated with feelings of cheerfulness and enthusiasm and is responsible for fuelling the energy required to increase our motivational level to get things done.

'Now tell me about a time when you were really down in the dumps—really unhappy,' said the consultant. After some thought and visible hesitation, Radha described a personal experience from around two years ago. Radha had been married for a few years when she noticed that her husband, Vikas, would come home very late and only to sleep. At first, she believed that since Vikas had set up a new business it was only natural that he needed to keep long hours. She soon realised, however, that it was not the long hours that really bothered her—it was his lack of interest in their relationship.

In the meantime, Radha became pregnant with her first child, and although Vikas did not seem to share her joy, she hoped that things would turn around soon. In her eighth month of pregnancy, she discovered that her husband was involved in a relationship with the office assistant—a young girl he had hired a couple of years ago. So much so, they had created a small living space in the office, which they stayed in whenever he claimed to be travelling.

Unimaginable shock, rejection and helplessness followed. Radha wept uncontrollably for days and begged her husband to give up his relationship with his assistant, even threatening to take her life if he did not. But it was to no avail. The only hope that kept her going was the forthcoming birth of her baby. The next six months brought joy and hopelessness at the same time. The love she received from her daughter was in sharp contrast to the indifference she experienced from her husband.

Slowly, Radha accepted that her marriage was over.

Through the support of her friends, she went back to the company where she was working—being lucky to get back a familiar job. She worked hard; after all, she owed it to her daughter. Besides, she had no choice—she had to support them both. However, she did not resent this fact. Radha's work made her forget the personal anguish and pain she was going through. In the past year and a half, she had received great feedback from her supervisor and had been promoted recently. 'Yes, it has been tough—but now I am happy,' Radha concluded.

> Contented people are in control of their lives. Discontented people, however, are overcome by feelings of sadness and a general lack of energy and drive to do things. They have a tendency to worry about the future. In more severe cases, they tend to feel chronically guilty and dissatisfied with their lives; they withdraw socially and sometimes even entertain suicidal thoughts.

'As happy as the time when you were a schoolgirl?' the consultant persisted.

Expectedly, Radha broke into tears, expressing how her life had changed. She often felt worthless, even if she was doing well. Except for her work and her daughter, she had no time for anything else and had forgotten the ability to enjoy herself. Her weekends were spent planning for the week and attending to her daughter—often she felt mechanical as she went about her life. 'No, I'm not content. You're right. Something nags at me all the time. There's something missing.'

Sometimes, we take action to improve our circumstances, but we may still not be happy. This lingering unhappiness often resurfaces at a later time, getting in the way of high contentment. Radha has taken action but has given up on herself and is leading a very mechanical life. Thus, despite the fact that she is doing everything right, she is not leading a joyful, contented life. This could be because she does not know what will bring her joy.

Recognising what was happening to her, Radha asked the consultant, 'What should I do? I think I need help.'

Behind the Scenes

In the above story, Radha went to great lengths to change her life for the better. She got out of a bad marriage and made an effort to live a happy, independent life, energised by her daughter's love. While she was happier at this time than she had been in her marriage, she had not fully overcome the negativity of her relationship with her husband. She was still carrying the feelings of rejection and helplessness and dealing with the Herculean task of being a single mother. Her life revolved around providing for her daughter. Juggling work and childcare left Radha little time and energy for herself. Also, the negative memories of her first marriage made it difficult for her to enjoy her present. There was an immense sense of loneliness that made her unable to give her best and realise her potential.

It is important for Radha to set apart some leisure time to spend on her likes, her hobbies or with people she enjoys. Speaking to old friends or making new friends could help her overcome her past and find new anchors and goals in life. Contented people like and accept themselves, which translates into positive self-esteem and self-confidence. They feel good and at ease both at home and at work, and they make opportunities for having fun. They are not overly obsessed with work and enjoy their leisure time.

Contented people are also less self-focused, less hostile and abusive and less susceptible to ill health than others. Generally, they function well emotionally and socially and perform very well on the job, particularly when interacting with internal and external customers. Surveys have shown that contentment is very important in building high-performance teams.

TOOLBOX   Striving for Joy

Allocate time to spend on things and people you enjoy.

People or things you enjoy	When will you spend time on these next?

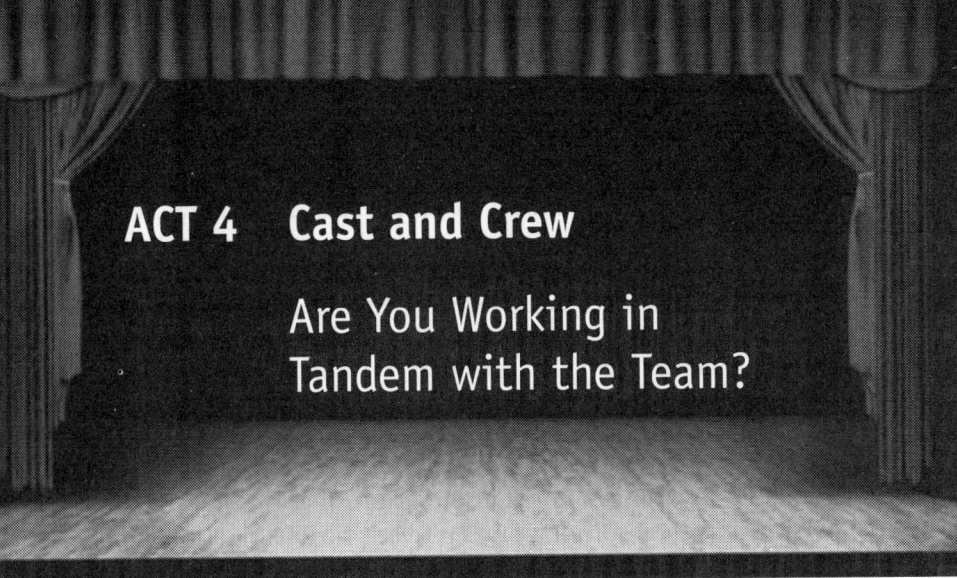

ACT 4 Cast and Crew

Are You Working in Tandem with the Team?

Social Awareness

'If your emotional abilities aren't in hand, if you don't have self-awareness, if you are not able to manage your distressing emotions, if you can't have empathy and have effective relationships, then no matter how smart you are, you are not going to get very far.'
~ Daniel Goleman

INTRODUCTION TO SOCIAL AWARENESS

In the previous chapters, we have looked at the various facets that are key to knowing oneself—self-awareness, self-management and self-motivation. We have explored what makes us tick and faced the root of our emotions and motivation. Let us also look beyond ourselves to the other—to our relationships with the people in our life.

Just as the interplay between protagonists creates the dramas in the stage of theatre, the interactions between people in their personal and professional lives create the dramas of life.

As Mahatma Gandhi once said:

It is man's social nature which distinguishes him from the brute creation. If it is his privilege to be independent, it is equally his duty to be inter-dependent. Only an arrogant man will claim to be independent of everybody else and be self-contained.

Social awareness is the foundation of how successfully we manage these dramas and cultivate various relationships. However, cultivating strong relationships goes beyond simply communicating well with others. It is not only about how eloquently you speak or write, or how intelligently you convey your ideas through memos and speeches—rather, it is the unspoken communication of the emotional flow and trust between people that determines the brilliance of their relationships.

Therefore, at the core of social awareness lies:

- *Empathy*: recognising, understanding and appreciating others' feelings, needs and concerns.
- *Trust*: believing in the reliability and ability of other people, and building relationships based on integrity.

In this chapter, we will explore these concepts through real-life stories. These stories will be followed by exercises that help you tangibly apply the concept of social awareness to your particular experiences and situation.

Reaching Out and Creating Connections

MRS NAMBIAR'S STORY: THE MYSTERY OF THE E-SAT SCORES

In February 2011, after a year of intense meetings and discussions, the board of directors of Banking International made a difficult decision. They decided that it was time to make radical cutbacks and shut down the Chennai branch of their business. The managing director (MD) of Banking International, Mr Shroff, asked the head of the southern unit, Mrs Nambiar, to handle the transition until the closing day in September 2011. This meant that Mrs Nambiar was responsible for communicating the harsh message to all the employees at the Chennai branch, as well as for getting the team to complete all their pending tasks. In addition, she was to handle the paperwork and formalities until Mr Shroff arrived from the head office in September. She was also to prepare for her own shift to the head office.

In July 2011, the company carried out an organisation-wide employee satisfaction survey. As per the procedure, all units, including the Chennai branch of the company, were included in the survey. When Mr Shroff learnt of this, he asked the HR department to consolidate and send the results of the Chennai branch to him, fearing the worst. Tentatively, he clicked on the Excel sheet sent to him to see what the branch had to say. Seeing the results, his eyes widened and his jaw dropped. A surprisingly large number of people had rated satisfaction as 4 on 5. The overall scores indicated 76 per cent employee satisfaction (E-SAT). Where Mr Shroff had expected a major drop in the E-SAT scores, there was instead a marginal increase from the previous year! In fact, the Chennai branch was the only unit that showed such high levels of E-SAT.

Suspicious of the report and scores, Mr Shroff contacted HR and looked more closely at the score sheets. Unable to find any deviance there, he decided to investigate the scene himself. He called Mrs Nambiar and questioned her closely about the results. Mrs Nambiar calmly acknowledged his surprise and, at the same time, assured him that they were based on the employees' true feelings. She invited him to speak to her people when he was in town next. Mr Shroff expressed his eagerness to see how Mrs Nambiar was handling the situation.

> Empathy is the ability to recognise, understand and appreciate the feelings of others. It is being sensitive to what, how and why people feel the way they do. Highly empathetic people often make good facilitators and negotiators because empathy is a critical factor in communication with others. This skill is very desirable in business interactions, especially when aiming at win–win situations.

Mr Shroff's curiosity drove him to advance his visit by a month, and August 2011 found Mr Shroff in Chennai. What he saw surprised him. The employees truly seemed positive and motivated. He spent time with Mrs Nambiar to understand what was driving their contentment. While she could not pinpoint any single reason, he made a few observations of his own.

Mr Shroff found that every morning Mrs Nambiar greeted each team member as she walked into office. She took time to drop by their desks and speak to them and, more importantly, listen to each and every staff member. She asked them how they were doing, how their job hunt was going and how their family was adjusting to the bad news. She heard their responses and sometimes gave them suggestions on how to handle the tough situation. Mrs Nambiar ensured that people in the division had an opportunity to express their anxieties, anger, frustrations and self-doubts. Often, through these sessions, she would re-direct the conversations towards helping people explore their skills and build confidence in their abilities to get past this tough situation.

> Highly empathetic people are considerate and concerned about people in general. They listen well and respond to the needs expressed by others. They offer useful feedback wherever possible and tend to inspire people to bring out their best. Empathy works hand in hand with trust and is at the core of the concept of emotional intelligence, representing a critical component of social awareness. Pay special note to how Mrs Nambiar gains the trust of her employees by encouraging them to speak freely and by empathising with their concerns.

Mrs Nambiar would also encourage people to share their experiences in team meetings, building a learning and sharing environment where they found great support. Wherever possible, she used a few of her personal contacts to assist them in their job hunt. Mr Shroff instantly realised that her keen listening skills and extreme empathy towards her people made them feel cared for, engaged and optimistic. No wonder the E-SAT scores demonstrated this.

The most significant learning for Mr Shroff was that when chips are down, people want to know the truth. It is not 'knowing the bad news' that concerns them as much as the way with which this news is communicated to them. The staff possibly understood the decision for closure, even though they may not have liked it—what mattered more was that Mrs Nambiar was a boss who listened to their concerns and provided all the emotional support and help people needed to move on.

> Empathy allows us to 'read' others as events transpire, receive interpersonal input and adjust our actions accordingly for maximum effect. People who are highly empathetic are well suited for leadership positions and jobs where human relations are critical, for example, in customer service, health care, education, sales and management.

At the end of his trip, Mr Shroff asked Mrs Nambiar if they could speak about this. He explained what he had seen and greatly appreciated her emotional skills. He marvelled at the fact that she took time out to speak to her staff despite the million formalities she had to complete, and especially when there was no clear benefit in it for her. Mrs Nambiar explained that she had learned the value of empathy through a personal experience.

Three years ago, her husband had been in a position similar to that of her people now. He was assigned to work on a large proposal that would lead to a major account for the company. He struggled hard and the company invested large sums to meet the order. While pressure to succeed began building up, her husband stuck through it all, knowing that his efforts would soon bear fruit. However, the company lost the proposal to a competitor and suffered a major loss. Suddenly, without warning, he was asked to resign by the CEO. His instant reaction was disbelief and that gave way to intense rage. The only reason he was able to get past that rage, as Mrs Nambiar explained, was because of his boss. After the meeting with the CEO, his boss called him into his cabin and explained the reasons behind the lay-off. He appreciated Mr Nambiar's efforts and explained how he had added value to the project and to the company as a whole. He expressed confidence in his ability to find another job. He not only wrote a glowing reference but also recommended him to a few of his friends in other organisations. It was only with his help that Mr Nambiar was able to get over the unfortunate incident and move on to greener pastures.

> Lack of empathy, to a large extent, comes from the absence of 'listening' and 'probing'. It is essential to develop these skills if empathy is to be improved at all. The power of empathy is key to get people to overcome their worst problems.

With this background, Mr Shroff better understood Mrs Nambiar's behaviour. He decided to actively practise being empathetic in Chandigarh. The business situation in the Chandigarh office was similar to Chennai, with the office on the verge of being shut down. However, in the absence of an empathetic boss, such as Mrs Nambiar, the Chandigarh employees were far more disgruntled than their counterparts in Chennai. As a first step, Mr Shroff called a conference the following week and explained the company's situation and why the unit was being shut. He then invited people to talk about how they felt about the situation. Initially, he was scared of the reactions he would get, but he persevered. Prone to jumping to provide solutions, Mr Shroff had to exercise extra effort to simply listen and understand what they were saying.

There were a few people who were angry and felt that the decision was unfair. Mr Shroff did not attempt to justify or defend himself. He allowed others to express their emotions without any judgement. His openness to listening to their viewpoints perhaps made them appreciate the fact that he was valuing them and being honest with them. Through the following days, he spent time with each person, acknowledging their hurdles and exploring ways to find a solution.

At the end of his Chandigarh visit, Mr Shroff knew he was a changed man.

Behind the Scenes

As seen in Mrs Nambiar's story, true caring or empathy is always about the other person's feelings, views, beliefs and compulsions. In moving from agony to ecstasy in relationships, empathy can only work when we are aware of ourselves, manage our inner voices and then listen to the other person with respect and openness. The point at which the other person believes and feels that 'I have been understood and I matter' is when a deep bond gets created—often described as an emotional connect.

In this way, empathy is a very desirable skill in business interactions, especially when aiming at win–win scenarios. Individuals and groups high in empathy are adept at judging people's needs and understanding what is important to the other party. They can structure deals so that the other party feels they have received something in return for what they gave. This plays an important role in the success of certain transactions, such as mergers, for example.

TIPS AND TRICKS   Understanding Empathy

1. Getting work done and getting work done through engagement are two different things. Logic is not the only way in which people process information; they also need to work through and understand their emotions when dealing with difficult news. However, many managers often feel that working on and through the emotions of others is time-consuming and sometimes emotionally draining. This is why, perhaps, everyone is not cut out to be a leader—for leaders will enjoy the people processes, of which empathy is the key.

2. Empathy is not only a 'soft' skill that means being nice. Of course, the views of the other person and a respect for differences are inherent in the 'empathic process', but empathy is also about 'tough love'. This is why it is described as an emotional skill that requires courage.

3. In situations of high stress, people need to talk out their problems with someone who is non-evaluative and non-judgemental. Once they have emotionally moved past the trauma, they are able to focus on problem-solving. When people feel they are heard, they develop a sense of faith in the person or organisation. They are more likely to express new ideas and innovative solutions. Encouraging people to speak up improves the quality of team interactions. Thus, empathy is an important skill for a leader to derive the best from his or her team.

TOOLBOX   Empathy

Techniques for improving your listening:

- Make sure to feel accepting enough to be able to focus on the speaker's point.
- Focus on the needs of the other person.
- Use non-judgmental words, avoid labelling.
- Be a good friend to silence.
- Start noticing when you are not listening anymore.

SCENE 2

The Power of True Communication

SOHINI'S STORY: BURNING BRIDGES INSTEAD OF BUILDING THEM

When Sohini joined MediaNow (a small magazine company in Kolkata) as a salesperson, she was given a target of bringing in 51 new customers each quarter, from institutions such as hotels and hospitals. For the first three months, she worked very hard to meet her targets. Sohini's special expertise lay in arranging for follow-up meetings after the sale to ensure that all of her customers were satisfied. At this point, she would usually get a repeat order, or references for other potential clients.

While preparing for the end of quarter review, Sohini realised that she had actually brought in 55 new customers and also had more in the pipeline. The sales head in the east region had quit two weeks before the quarter end. In the light of her performance and being the next in line, Sohini saw his exit as an opportunity for her to step up. She was extremely excited and counted the minutes until her review.

In her review, Mr Gokhale commended Sohini's target achievement but told her off for not following processes. Her job was to make a sale; she should not have spent as much time in follow-up meetings. She tried to explain her point of view, but Mr Gokhale countered that with the fact that she could have used that time to identify even more customers. Additionally, he felt that the target was not a stretch for her and politely asked if she would be willing to increase it to 60. Sohini had no choice but to agree. She walked out of the room, dejected. This was not how she had imagined the discussion would go.

A few weeks down the line, Sohini was once again caught up in the whirlwind of sales numbers and client meetings. In the absence of a sales head, it was a little more difficult to meet her targets, but as a senior salesperson, she tried to not let it affect her.

Then, one Monday morning, there was a new face in the office. Sohini was caught off guard as she had had no idea that someone else was joining the sales team. She politely stepped up and introduced herself. The new person's name was Ragini, and she turned out to be the new sales head. Sohini was shocked—no one had informed her about this development. She learned that Ragini had the same number of years of experience as her, and had never previously handled sales. Almost immediately, Sohini found herself resenting Ragini.

> Perhaps unsurprisingly, Sohini is predisposed to resent Ragini. She does not seem to consider the fact that Ragini herself has little to do with the organisational decision to not promote Sohini. Instead of overcoming her initial feelings and building a relationship based on trust and open communication with her new sales head, Sohini chooses to go in a different direction. Pay special note to Sohini's reaction to the situation—how would you go about resolving such an issue?

Over the next week, Sohini was expected to give Ragini a download of all the information that she had—the sales process at MediaNow, key clients, competitors to watch out for and so on. Sohini also took Ragini out for a few client calls for her to learn the ropes. She found herself disliking Ragini more and more, as she happily told anyone who would ask her.

Two weeks in, Ragini was still only 'supporting' Sohini on client calls—she would sit quietly while Sohini did all the talking. When they got back to office, Mr Gokhale would call Ragini and she would report on everything that was discussed in the meeting. Sohini felt that Ragini was stealing her limelight; to add insult to injury, she was also making more money than her! Slowly, Sohini felt less inclined to make an effort. She reduced the number of calls she made, and she pushed Ragini to lead all meetings that they went to. Ragini's inexperience, clubbed with Sohini's unwillingness, made sales in the Kolkata region suffer greatly. In addition, Sohini increasingly began to speak ill of Ragini behind her back. Soon, people in other locations also began to think of Ragini as incompetent.

> Building trust involves exposing our vulnerabilities, while mistrust stems mainly from inadequate communication and problems that are not addressed. Sohini is unwilling to believe that Ragini will not take advantage of the situation. Rather than placing her trust in Ragini, or having an open conversation with her or Mr Gokhale, Sohini resorts to rumour-mongering—a tactic that often chips away at the reputation of the gossiper herself/himself.

Fed up, Sohini started looking out for a new job, often pretending to head out for 'meetings' that were actually interviews. Soon an opportunity presented itself—it was with an organisation called NewTimes, which was a direct competitor to MediaNow. The opportunity seemed perfect, but they wanted her to join the following week. Just a week before she was to be confirmed, Sohini quit giving three days of notice. She knew she would be leaving MediaNow high and dry as it would take them some time to get another person on board and Ragini did not have all the relevant client databases or updates.

Rather than feel bad about it, Sohini used this fact to her advantage. Bitter about the way things had turned out at MediaNow, she began reaching out to all of her previous clients. She felt that their loyalty lay with her rather than with MediaNow, since she was the one who had ensured that they were satisfied.

When the team at MediaNow found out, they immediately rose to take legal action against Sohini. However, she knew she would be safe, as she was still not confirmed by the organisation. Despite this, some of her clients began to doubt her integrity. Sohini's ill will towards Ragini was well known by now, and her actions seemed driven by a personal vendetta. With MediaNow joining forces with these clients to criticise her approach, Sohini's reputation in Kolkata's media circles took a hit. Not only did she fail to engage with some of her previous clients, a number of NewTimes' existing clients also refused to work with her.

> It takes years of careful work to create a reputation. Sohini's actions cause her clients to question her integrity and loyalty—values that are key to a successful professional relationship.

Thus, Sohini's vengeful act, born out of mutual distrust, ruined seven years' worth of hard work that had gone into building a name for herself.

Whether Sohini was the villain or the victim is a matter of perspective.

Behind the Scenes

Trust is a key aspect of healthy relationships between people, be it within or outside organisations. At an emotional level, trust means exposing our vulnerabilities and believing that the other will not take advantage of our openness, while enabling the other to do the same.

For employees to be motivated and engaged, it is important that the organisation and workforce trust each other to make fair decisions, behave with integrity and see themselves as valued members of a worthy community. Despite knowing this, many companies, workforce and colleagues view each other with profound distrust. Why is this?

Trust is a complex and fragile construct as it involves exposing our vulnerabilities and having little control over the outcome—many of us find this very difficult to do. Trust is hard to build, but easy to destroy. It can take aeons to build a reputation for fairness and consistency; however, this image can be shattered with a single move, such as in the case of Sohini.

Another obstacle to trust-building is the fact that a number of managers believe that they can achieve greater efficiency and maintain a power balance by controlling employees and keeping them at a safe distance; they thus refrain from engaging in trusting relationships with their team members.

Given these challenges, it is no surprise that building, maintaining and repairing trust are amongst an organisation's most daunting tasks. Yet, trust is the basis of success for high-performing leaders who have faith that their people will do their best and work for the greater organisational goals. Faith enables employees to resolve disagreements, take smarter risks, stay with the company longer and contribute better ideas. Without it, people disengage from their work, focus on rumours and politics and begin looking elsewhere for a job. As we see in Sohini's story, her lack of trust in the organisation and in Ragini causes her to look for another job and leave on unpleasant terms.

Mistrust stems mainly from inadequate communication, misbehaviour and problems that have not been remedied or addressed. Factors such as endless reorganisation, volatile leaders, scapegoating or a history of underperformance are also amongst the enemies of trust.

Inconsistent messages and false feedback too contribute to a culture of mistrust. One of the ways to ensure that you are giving the right messages is to perceive what your audience is expressing non-verbally and responding to both the verbal and non-verbal messages. This is where empathy— the ability to pay attention to emotional cues and understand others well—comes in, a concept we discussed in the previous section.

Know More: The Secret of Their Success? Trust

The business case for trust has never been stronger. In their book, *Smart Trust*, Stephen M.R. Covey, Greg Link and Rebecca Merrill give real-life examples of companies where trust is the foundation of success. In their words, 'More and more it is becoming abundantly evident that in today's economy, the bottom line is directly connected to trust. Put another way, there is a "business case for trust"—and it's a compelling case.'

However, the authors explain that it cannot be blind trust. Rather, it has to be 'smart trust', which uses analysis to make sure trust does not go awry—in this way, some of the world's most successful companies display a high propensity to trust combined with an equally high analysis. (Excerpts below provided from *The Globe and Mail*.)

eBay Inc.: 'When Pierre Omidyar founded eBay Inc. it was an unlikely candidate for business success, given that it brought together buyers and sellers from around the world who would conduct single transactions without knowing each other. Suspicion and distrust seemed a huge barrier. But Mr Omidyar believed that most people are basically good and could be trusted, and the site flourished.'

(Continued)

(Continued)

> *Grameen Bank:* 'When Muhammad Yunus founded Grameen Bank, he was also making a bet on humanity's inherent trustworthiness. He lent money to people who nobody else would dream of giving money to: impoverished individuals with no collateral, no steady employment, and no verifiable credit history. But in the end repayment rates at his bank were significantly higher than traditional banking loans.'
>
> *Berkshire Hathaway:* 'When Warren Buffett buys a new business for his Berkshire Hathaway empire, he places his trust in the executives of the company he is taking over. Rather than dismissing them immediately, or easing them out after a short interval, as so many other firms do after acquisitions, he only buys companies with executives he would want to keep and then leaves them alone—trusting them to make money for him. Mr Buffett's headquarters staff is only about 20 people, who oversee 77 operating companies and 257,000 employees, a sign of the trust in the leaders of those companies.'

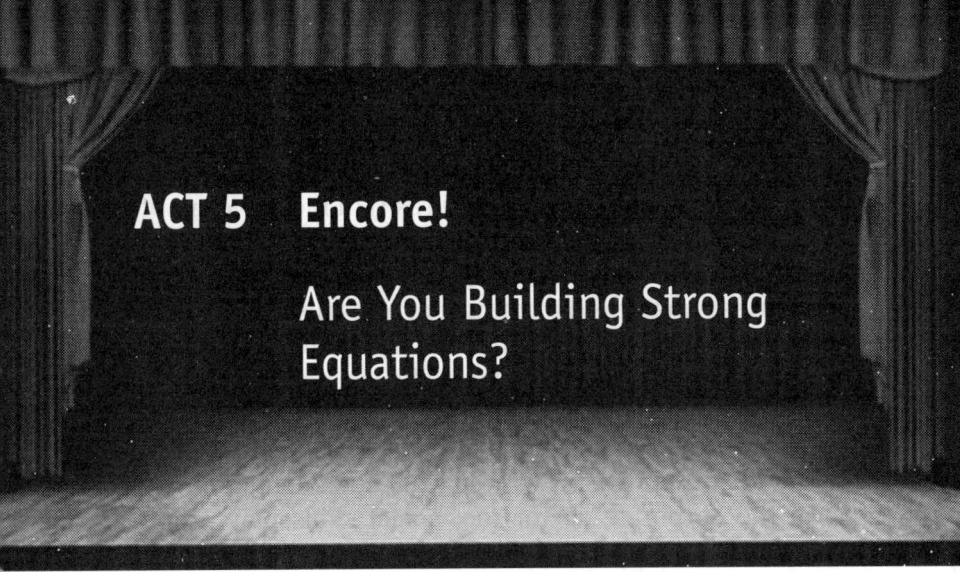

ACT 5 Encore!

Are You Building Strong Equations?

INTRODUCTION TO SOCIAL SKILLS

'He's good with people—he knows how to get the best out of them.' 'She has excellent people skills—everyone likes and respects her!' 'He inspires so much loyalty in his team.' 'Clients trust her judgement completely.'

You must have heard one or more variations of these statements—either in your time in the corporate world or in the personal sphere. This concept is more familiar to countries with high-context work cultures (such as India) than low-context work cultures. (Refer to Edward Hall's work on high- and low-context work cultures.[1]) In India, we are often told about the importance of building loyalty, forging relationships and being a team player. In many traditional Indian industries, business is contingent on trust and personal interaction. Take, for example, the diamond traders of Surat or the garment traders of Old Delhi—in both sectors, businessmen create strong relationships over years and lakhs of rupees worth of transactions take place on the basis of word of mouth, often without written legal documentation.

In the corporate sector too, social skills play a crucial role. Put simply, social skills refer to the competence needed to get along with other people and to establish good relationships with them. Social skills are, to a large extent, based on empathy. Listening carefully to other people and responding to interpersonal cues are integral to effective social interaction.

People who master social skills do well at everything that requires full interaction with other people: sales, management, negotiation, communication, teaching, raising a family, motivation, inspiration, team-building and so on. These skills are key to any kind of partnership—business or personal.

In this chapter, we will explore the two components of social skills:

- *Interpersonal relations*: Establishing and maintaining relationships.
- *Group orientation*: Feeling part of a group and being a co-operative and contributing member.

Each of these components will be illustrated through stories of people dealing with social skills issues in their everyday life. The stories will be followed by exercises and tips that will help you tangibly apply the concept of social skills to your particular experiences and situation.

---

[1] Hall, Edward, T. *Beyond Culture*. New York: Anchor Books (7 December 1976). ISBN-10: 0385124740, ISBN-13: 978-0385124744.

SCENE 1

Building Bridges, Not Walls

SRISHTI'S STORY: LEADING A LIMITED, ISOLATED LIFE

Srishti had always felt a little different. Unlike the other children around her, she knew exactly what she wanted to be when she grew up—a leading economist, such as Amartya Sen. While her classmates were busy with birthday parties and cartoons, Srishti spent all her time studying. Her teachers praised her to the skies and her classmates looked up to her. It was no surprise when she topped her Class X and then her Class XII board exams. Srishti did have a few friends, but she was not considered popular. She longed to find more people like herself but felt that most of them were unintelligent and focused on frivolous things.

> Many of the lessons necessary for effective social behaviour are learned at a young age in group activities such as taking turns, co-operation, conflict resolution, working together for the good of the whole and dealing with failure and rejection. People have a natural tendency to withdraw if they are not encouraged to interact with others or face social difficulties at that vulnerable age.

Free to choose any course and any college she liked, Srishti chose to pursue a BA in Economics from Shri Ram College of Commerce (SRCC). She planned to complete her Bachelors in Delhi and then go to Trinity College, Cambridge. With her scores, she knew she had an excellent chance. When Srishti learned that universities abroad valued extra-curricular activities, she immediately signed up for the debating society. She tried to get into the Model UN Society too, as she was sure it would look good on her college application. However, it was an exclusive group that people were invited to by word of mouth, and Srishti could not figure out how to get in.

In her first year at SRCC, Srishti ignored invitations to the freshers' dance and numerous college fests. She felt that her time was better spent reading at home. To get admission into Trinity, Srishti was willing to make a few sacrifices; the more time she spent studying, the more difficult she found it to be friends with any of her classmates. She could not connect with them at all. If she missed a class, she would have a hard time getting notes. But it did not really matter; Srishti would ace the paper anyway. Besides, she believed that when she got to Trinity, she would find more like-minded people to interact with.

> Interpersonal relations refer to the ability to establish and maintain mutually satisfying relationships characterised by emotional closeness, intimacy and by the capacity to give and receive affection. Srishti is ambitious and goal oriented—but she does not possess or cultivate the art of forming connections with people around her. Instead, she isolates herself, maintaining a singular focus on academia.

One day, as Srishti walked down the road dreaming about Trinity, she noticed a car zooming past her. At the wheel was Farhan, laughing and talking with a large group of friends crammed into his car.

Farhan was one of Srishti's classmates from school. Although Srishti was not very interested in her classmates in general, she could not help but notice Farhan. It seemed that everywhere Farhan went, he attracted a crowd. He was warm and friendly—nice to everyone he met and oozing with loads of charm. Farhan was not good at studies, mostly because he spent little time studying. Yet he had the uncanny ability to talk his way out of just about any type of situation. In Class XII, Farhan had been elected school captain and was voted 'Mr Popular' at the farewell. Farhan managed to score average marks in his board exams. Armed with his natural charisma and an extensive list of extra-curricular activities, he was admitted to the prestigious St Stephens College and joined both the college sports club and the Shakespeare Society.

> Interpersonal skill is associated with the ability to feel at ease in the presence of others, to look forward to social encounters and to be sensitive to others' needs. Farhan has a high social quotient; he is cheerful and fun to be around. Pay special note to how social interactions (and the lack thereof) play a key role in the lives of Farhan and Srishti.

Srishti managed to get into her dream college, Trinity. Two years later, she aced her postgraduation class and decided to study further in London and complete her PhD. She was neck deep in her PhD at the University of London when her parents decided it was time she settled down. She got married and soon had a daughter. Sadly, within the short span of three years, her marriage ended. Her husband described her as someone 'cold and distant—not in the least interested in people'. It was not that she was an introvert—she simply had neither the time nor the energy to be interested in and take care of another person. Even with her daughter, her involvement was minimal. Srishti was so involved in her research that she would frequently stay the night at the library, often having her first meal of the day at three in the afternoon. Her concerned parents moved to London to help her take care of her daughter. Srishti had spent so much of her life with books that she now had a difficult time relating to other people. Books were her only friends.

> Never having learned the art of building and sustaining relationships, Srishti is unable to create intimacy in the spheres of marriage and parenthood.

Meanwhile, Farhan started his own garment export business after college. With help from an uncle who was based in London, Farhan began his export business. With his natural flair for networking and connecting with people, he became a successful entrepreneur. With support from his cousin and uncle, he moved to London permanently and set up operations there. His social aptitude enabled him to find more customers and expand his business. He married his college sweetheart and lived with his wife and two children in the same neighbourhood as Srishti. He was still in touch with his old friends and was instrumental in organising their school and college reunions in the city.

Despite living in the same neighbourhood, Srishti and Farhan never crossed paths. While Farhan remained gregarious and had a number of friends even in his new city, Srishti only stepped out when absolutely necessary. In fact, Srishti did not even know the names of her next-door neighbours.

Behind the Scenes

Whose life seems more fulfilling—Farhan's or Srishti's? Their contrasting stories demonstrate how interpersonal skills can create different dramas and endings in people's lives.

Most people would agree that Farhan's life seems ideal; he achieved professional success and was surrounded by friends and family. Srishti, despite her education and IQ, did not manage to succeed in her relationships—she ended up alone and friendless. Srishti valued education and ambition above relationships from the very beginning. Perhaps that is why all she was left with in life was her research.

What Farhan lacked in conventional IQ, he made up for by way of social skills. Despite being an average performer in school, he managed to make it to one of the most coveted colleges in the country. He made for pleasant company and, as a result, had a large number of friends. His social skills extended to his family as well. His uncle supported his entrepreneurship, and Farhan ultimately had a fulfilling life—complete with loved ones and a booming career.

All of us need social interactions to help us navigate successfully through our personal and professional lives. We need the love, approval, support and care of our near and dear ones to be successful. Mutually satisfying relationships include meaningful social interchanges that are potentially rewarding and enjoyable. Positive interpersonal relationships are characterised by the ability to give and receive warmth and affection and convey intimacy to another person. People with strong interpersonal skills are often described as extroverts. They are able to recognise and respond to social cues and show genuine concern for others.

People with high IQ or educational qualifications are highly respected. However, if they lack basic social skills, their success could be limited to their field of expertise. Overall success requires social skills as much as intellectual capabilities—sometimes even more.

Interpersonal relations are of prime importance for people in customer-facing or sales roles. They are also an important prerequisite for climbing up the corporate ladder. People do not always have to be highly educated in order to be liked and to be successful. The late American president, Ronald Reagan, did not have the education of many of his colleagues in politics, but he was able to run rings around them when it came to charm. And it was his charm that made him one of the most successful presidents of the 20th century.

TOOLBOX   Interpersonal Skills Indicator

There are no right or wrong answers in this quiz. The more truthful you are, the more helpful it will be. You will not be asked to show your answers to anyone unless you are willing to do so.

Read through the list of some of the skills we use when we try to get on with other people. Place a tick in the box which describes how good or bad you are at that skill.

1. Starting talking to someone you know	Very Bad	Bad	Average	Good	Very Good
2. Starting talking to someone you don't know	Very Bad	Bad	Average	Good	Very Good
3. Keeping a conversation going	Very Bad	Bad	Average	Good	Very Good
4. Asking someone to explain something you have not understood	Very Bad	Bad	Average	Good	Very Good
5. Listening to what others say	Very Bad	Bad	Average	Good	Very Good
6. Saying what you feel	Very Bad	Bad	Average	Good	Very Good
7. Standing up for what you believe in	Very Bad	Bad	Average	Good	Very Good
8. Saying sorry	Very Bad	Bad	Average	Good	Very Good
9. Asking for information, e.g., what time is the next bus	Very Bad	Bad	Average	Good	Very Good

10. Asking for someone to leave you alone	Very Bad	Bad	Average	Good	Very Good
11. Saying thank you	Very Bad	Bad	Average	Good	Very Good
12. Speaking in front of a group	Very Bad	Bad	Average	Good	Very Good
13. Speaking to someone of the same sex	Very Bad	Bad	Average	Good	Very Good
14. Speaking to someone of the opposite sex	Very Bad	Bad	Average	Good	Very Good
15. Making a complaint	Very Bad	Bad	Average	Good	Very Good
16. Keeping your temper	Very Bad	Bad	Average	Good	Very Good
17. Speaking on the telephone	Very Bad	Bad	Average	Good	Very Good
18. Speaking to older people	Very Bad	Bad	Average	Good	Very Good
19. Speaking to younger people	Very Bad	Bad	Average	Good	Very Good
20. Knowing when to call people by their first name or Mr/Mrs	Very Bad	Bad	Average	Good	Very Good

How to interpret your results: If you scored Good/Very Good on:

- *15 or more items*—Congratulations! It appears you have a great ability to connect with others and thrive in social situations.
- *7–15 items*—You are probably comfortable in some situations, but struggle in others. Look more closely at

where you lost scores and create a plan to improve those areas.

- *Less than 7 items*—You may need to make some changes in the way you interact with people around you. Practice makes perfect, so schedule more time around other people, paying special attention to how they respond to you, and the emotions your words create on them. You could also plan a few conversations—for example, how to ask a stranger for directions, or how to start a conversation with a colleague—beforehand. Do not shy away from seeking help from someone you consider an expert.

Know More: Interpersonal Intelligence

In the1980s, American developmental psychologist Howard Gardner's path-breaking research focused on the fact that IQ is not the only intelligence required to be successful. In fact, Gardner concluded that there are multiple intelligences that make us successful, including interpersonal intelligence.

Interpersonal intelligence is concerned with the capacity to recognise and understand the moods, intentions, motivations and desires of other people. It allows people to work effectively with others. Individuals who have high interpersonal intelligence are characterised by their sensitivity to others and their ability to co-operate in order to work as part of a group.

Gardner believes this intelligence is particularly helpful for people in sales, politicians, managers, teachers, counsellors and social workers.

Becoming Part of a Larger Whole

Group Orientation

'The strength of the team is each individual member. The strength of each member is the team.'

~ Phil Jackson

ABHIJIT'S STORY: LEARNING TO BE A TEAM PLAYER

For the second year in a row, Xenon Associates' business was showing declining trends, even though the usual assumptions had been validated at the beginning of the year and Abhijit had intelligently crafted a strategy along with his top team to ensure a 20 per cent increase—by all means, an achievable target.

The promoters were somewhat concerned—even though Xenon had shown a 5 per cent growth in the last two years, this was nowhere near the 20 per cent promised. Abhijit had been brought in by the promoters as he had had an impeccable track record in his past two organisations. All of 42 years old, Abhijit was that rare combination of a strategic thinker and a strong implementer. The industry recognised him for his sound knowledge, his impressive network and, of course, his many successes. When Abhijit joined Xenon three years back, competition and employees alike were sure that very soon the company would become the benchmark for all to emulate. The first year, true to promise, was an on-plan performance—but the next two years told a different story.

As Abhijit studied the market reports one Sunday afternoon, he was very troubled to see the growth trends of the competitors for the year. Something had to be done, he knew, and urgently.

First thing Monday morning, he set up a half-day meeting at the end of the week with all his team members to brainstorm together about what they thought could be holding them back and what needed to be done now. Abhijit believed that working together with his team was one of his biggest strengths as a leader. Far too often, he had seen silo behaviours limit individuals and organisations alike. He also knew that the root cause of this attitude was not that people were bad; the dynamics of survival in a competitive world invariably brought out 'I, me, myself' behaviours in most situations. To counter this, in his last three roles, Abhijit had initiated several projects for teams to come together, along with team performance-based bonuses for the top team. He practised this value with a passion, sparing no opportunities to talk about its importance and ensuring that he aligned his own behaviours to larger team goals.

> Abhijit clearly knows and understands the value of group orientation—the ability to be a part of a social group or team as a co-operative and contributing member.

One of the stories Abhijit often referred to was that of the well-known Intel guiding principle of debate, commit, communicate and deliver. This meant that while as an organisation Intel encouraged diversity and differing views, once a team or organisation decision was taken, there was total commitment to make things happen. Abhijit wanted Xenon to adopt a similar mindset.

Abhijit looked forward to the team meeting; he knew his team would have all the information and facts ready for discussion by then. The somewhat-apprehensive group met on a balmy Friday morning, unsure about what would emerge.

One thing that held the group together was a high level of trust. With that as a given, the team was sure that they could openly and fearlessly discuss their viewpoints, knowing that none of them would be dismissed by their leader or their colleagues.

One by one, the existing strategy points were reviewed against assumptions and current reality. Past information and industry data were reconciled to look at gaps and their possible causes.

Finally, the group began to review the policy of building products to attract the 18–24 years age group. Abhijit personally had led this idea and was a strong believer of this new initiative that he had started a year and a half back. This strategy was supposed to be the game changer in terms of building the company brand. The main technology-based product consisted of a bank of all possible career opportunities globally and provided a step-by-step process to help individuals plan out their careers. It was aligned to Xenon's vision of being the top provider of all education solutions. As resources were limited, only a small team of people had been assigned to support product development and marketing for this product. While the first six months had seemed promising, the last year had moved slowly. Feedback received from the customers during test marketing stages had not been encouraging, and the passion of the team was visibly low.

As discussions around this initiative proceeded, Abhijit noticed that many members of his team had differing views about the need for this product, the way it was being implemented and, most of all, the timing. Certain team members pointed out that the competition in the market had become fiercer and thus the product required a lot more focus. The team knew that since the new product was linked with a social cause, the pricing had been worked out accordingly. Abhijit had envisioned this product as a great benefit to millions of young people who struggle to find work. Somewhat hesitatingly, everyone put their views on the table, suggesting a deferment of this initiative to a more appropriate time.

Listening to his team, Abhijit went through an emotional struggle for the next few minutes. His decision to go along with his team was definite in his mind—aligning with them was what he had always propagated. However, giving up on his deep convictions was not easy. 'I will think this over on the weekend,' he told himself.

> Deferring to a team's views and letting go, especially in cases where emotional attachment to the issue is strong, is not easy. Even for Abhijit, who strongly believes in the ethos of taking people along, giving up his 'baby' is a problematic struggle. Pay special note to how Abhijit tries to resolve his dilemma.

Abhijit tried to consider the other ideas that had been raised. He knew that each of them had some merit, but he still felt that his idea was the best. He started to introspect and reflect on why he was so passionate about this initiative. He knew it stemmed from his personal struggles when he was 20 years old. He had experimented with a number of jobs before he was finally able to find his niche. While each job had added some value, he felt that he could have saved a lot of time if such a product had been available in his youth.

However, he thought, not every child was like him. Children today were much more focused and had a host of options to support their career planning. Also, his team had not rejected the idea, but they had just postponed the launch to a more appropriate time, and they had strong reasons to back this suggestion.

Abhijit knew that it would be difficult for him to work on other initiatives, but he understood it was important for him to break his attachment to this idea. He forced himself to think of the interests of the larger group and what would be the best path for them to adopt.

First thing on Monday morning, Abhijit sent his response to the entire team—the project launch had been deferred.

Behind the Scenes

People such as Abhijit, who are co-operative, contributing and constructive members, are geared towards helping others and have high group orientation. Such people genuinely care about others and respect people's feelings. They are generally good team players who are committed to overall team or organisational goals. In fact, they may be willing to let go of certain personal interests in favour of achieving a team goal.

Simply put, group orientation means the ability to be a part of a social group or team—working well with others, being productive in a team scenario and seeking other members' feedback and involvement. It means to act in a socially responsible manner, even though it may not offer personal benefits. It also means listening to the voice of conscience and upholding social rules. People who are not group oriented are typically known for being self-centred and could be prone to exploiting others for their own gain.

We see how Abhijit underwent internal turmoil when his team opposed an initiative close to his heart. The dilemma between our own views and the views of a collective group is one of the most interesting dramas that we go through in life. In the above story, unlike what we often witness, Abhijit's behaviour shows that he trusted others and was willing to let go of a personal goal in favour of a larger team objective. In corporate scenarios, 'know it all' managers suppress opinions in conflict with their own—tragically, often in scenarios when they are needed the most. Such managers force their decisions, blinkered by their limited views, on the entire team or company.

Giving up one's emotional agenda in the interest of a larger group agenda requires a somewhat selfless attitude, a strong self that does not feel lesser if the personal view is not accepted and a belief in a larger cause.

Emotional Intelligence in Action

In our day-to-day lives, we encounter complex situations that demand the use of a combination of emotional intelligence competencies. In our experience, lack of competence in any of the key emotional skills can often challenge us in the situation. Although we may manage to work out the situation rationally, results are not forthcoming without overcoming the emotional barriers. In this section, we look at some of these situations, once again through the lens of real stories, and decipher the competencies that are critical for the situation at hand.

EMOTIONAL INTELLIGENCE AND CHANGE

The Link between Emotional Intelligence and Change

The stories in this section illustrate two situations of change—first at an individual level and second at an organisational level. In both cases, the emotional intelligence competencies that come into play are adaptability, impulse control and self-appraisal.

As you read, try and identify the points at which the mastery or lack of emotional intelligence skills shapes the stories.

What would you do in such a situation? What strategies would you employ to overcome the obstacles that come up?

Mr Pradhan's Story: Paradigm Shift

As part of a work-shadowing assignment, Mr Pradhan, the CEO of a prominent insurance organisation, was observed by a certified consultant through the course of one entire work day. Mr Pradhan's day began at 9 a.m. sharp. While he replied to his mails, the consultant sat by him, accompanied him through the five meetings that were scheduled that day and joined him for lunch.

Mr Pradhan came across as a highly efficient manager. He was an inspirational figure, one that everyone in the organisation looked up to. The consultant noticed the CEO's ability to hold people in rapt attention when he spoke. He always had his eye on the larger goal and, at the same time, was able to address the smaller details and tactical issues as well. All his meetings ended with clarity on next steps, timelines and responsibilities. He was able to handle multiple priorities, delegate effectively and stay calm in the face of crisis. Yet, there was one thing that bothered the consultant.

In the feedback session at the end of the day, the consultant sat facing Mr Pradhan. They went through the events of the day, when the consultant said, 'Everything seemed perfect but there is one thing that concerns me.' Mr Pradhan greeted this statement with heightened curiosity. Conscious of the fact that he was being observed, he had put his best foot forward through the day's meetings. He wondered what could be missing. Unsure of what he would hear next, he asked the consultant to elaborate.

'I feel that all of the conversations today were focused on internal issues and processes. Through the many meetings and discussions, even though issues of increased profitability, strategy and so on were discussed, there was no reference to the customer. I am wondering if this is an aberration or could this indicate something? Frankly, I did not hear you mention the word "customer" even once.'

Mr Pradhan smiled weakly. He knew the consultant was right. He thanked him for the feedback and began to introspect, looking at the facts objectively.

This was not the first time he was hearing this.

Two weeks ago, a meeting had been called by the regulatory authority, where all insurance companies were represented by the top leadership. Amongst other things discussed, the insurance organisations were pulled up for their lack of customer focus. They were told that there were too many issues that customers were complaining of and reminded that insurance companies must not lose focus on the very customers who create their business.

Mr Pradhan thought back to his own organisation's strategy. The company was relatively new and had risen rapidly through the five years of its existence. Now, however, it had reached a plateau in its growth curve. Through the discussion with the consultant, Mr Pradhan realised that what had helped the organisation succeed in its initial phases would not be enough to sustain growth in the future.

Mr Pradhan decided it was time to take radical steps to support the progress of the organisation. He called a meeting of his management team, including the top 20–25 managers. As the first step, he had a detailed chat about customer focus with them and encouraged them to visit different parts of the country to meet real customers and check up on their real needs and satisfaction levels.

After a month of travelling around the country, the managers came back to the head office, armed with stories of their end customers: There was the old lady who kept her policy in a safe under lock and key after her husband turned 70; there was the young man who had moved to the city and proudly purchased an insurance policy for his parents; there was the family in Kutch who had to rely heavily on insurance after their house was destroyed in the earthquake. Each manager had met a number of customers. They spoke to the people to understand their situations, their requirements and whether these were being met through the insurance policies they had invested in.

Connecting directly with people from all walks of life was an eye-opening experience for these leaders. They were now able to visualise the customer, who was no longer a nameless, faceless entity—someone to be roped in to buy insurance. Through engagement with the end customers, the managers could visualise their real concerns and hence were eager to modify their strategy accordingly. So far, the company's focus had been on the sales agent; while servicing the internal customer was vital, the crucial link to the end customer was missing. This realisation created a paradigm shift. Mr Pradhan, along with the top leadership, immediately called for a change in the company's strategy. They launched an organisation-wide customer centricity initiative to integrate customer perspectives in all the company processes. Two years down the line, with customer centricity as the new mantra and adequate training to build skills in this area, the company went on to gain their desired position in the market.

As Mr Pradhan reviewed the company's latest glowing progress report, he smiled to himself and silently thanked the consultant who had emphasised the missing piece of the puzzle and prompted Mr Pradhan to take action and change the game.

Behind the Scenes

The key element in a change situation is adaptability—the ability to change on a dime when necessary. Mr Pradhan was quick to make changes in his strategy when evidence supported the need to change. He did not get mired in his original plan and was open to reviewing the focus on the customer's needs and starting an initiative to remedy any weaknesses.

In the above story, the CEO's self-awareness and self-appraisal are evident. Mr Pradhan was open to and appreciative of the feedback received. He demonstrated self-confidence even as he explored the change that was required. To identify the real changes needed and influence the team, he sent his top people on a quest for discovery. The managers made a sincere effort to empathise with the people they meet, which in turn changed their outlook of the customer and their strategy. The end result was the roll-out of an organisation-wide change, spurring the company on to greater success.

The aspect of impulse control is to be able to think long term and 'hold one's horses' in pursuit of something worthwhile. This component plays a critical role in being able to successfully go through the change journey, which invariably calls for considerable self-restraint and patience.

Sudha's Story: Outside the Box

Sudha, a graduate from a premier management institute, worked as a senior manager for a leading company in the manufacturing sector. A few months after she joined, the learning and organisational development (L&OD) department of her organisation initiated a fast-track development journey to develop employees who were recognised as having high potential. The company knew that investment in human capital could provide a distinct competitive advantage in an industry driven by numbers.

The company organised for an emotional quotient (EQ) assessment of the identified high-potential individuals, which included Sudha. Through an emotional quotient assessment, Sudha's score was found to be 84—falling in the average range. On most parameters, her scores were in the mid-range, demonstrating no distinct emotional competencies. The problem was the low score in the component of risk taking and adaptability.

When the consultant shared Sudha's profile with her during the feedback session, she was taken aback. She felt that the test was not accurate. She was aware of the link between emotional intelligence and leadership. She knew that the role of leaders is to enable their people to perform their best, appealing to people's feelings and instilling confidence in all stakeholders. How could her scores be just average? Surely, the test results did not reflect her true skills and personality.

The consultant explained the component of adaptability and probed on why she felt the result was inaccurate, asking her to give a few examples of how she may have responded in an adaptable manner in situations. Sudha explained that she had *adjusted* well to the various changes that the organisation had gone through. In fact, it was because of these qualities that the organisation had identified her as a high-potential employee.

By probing further, the consultant unearthed that Sudha tended to play by the book. She was extremely analytical and process-driven and was not quite willing to take risks. She found it difficult to deal with uncertainty or take a leap of faith—qualities that are critical to a senior leadership role. Understanding adaptability in this light, Sudha was reminded of a project that she had worked on last year. She was heading a new production unit. The unit worked well when it started off, but as it began to grow, Sudha discovered that the market demand was greater than they could supply. She desperately needed to find a way to increase production volumes—pronto. She managed to increase the supply slightly by handing out incentives for working overtime, but it was not nearly enough. Sudha went back to the management and informed them of the issues she was facing. Her unit was small with a handful of skilled workers. There was not much more she could do. She issued a statement informing the organisation of the maximum volumes she could produce. Her manager was dissatisfied with this approach and decided to step in. He discovered that by simply buying the technology for a part of the work that they currently outsourced, they could drastically reduce their production time and thus increase productivity. Sudha was amazed at this solution. She had never realised that buying the technology was an option. While it seemed like a big investment at the time, they would soon recover this cost. Sudha recalled that after that incident her manager had given her feedback, urging her to think up ways of adapting her strategy and taking risks to find the best solution for the organisation and the market.

Pondering over this incident, Sudha realised that she really could work on being more flexible in her thinking. She opened up to the consultant and became willing to listen. The consultant explained that there are many unknowns when dealing with the future, yet strategies have to be built and risks must be taken. Sudha was advised on how she could use her strengths to manage uncertainty.

Behind the Scenes

In the story above, Sudha found it difficult to think differently when dealing with changing circumstances. She liked to think within boundaries and constraints. She overestimated her ability to adapt and preferred to play safe. Sudha's story shows that she had trouble coming up with and adopting risky strategies. Her own statement on how she 'adapted' to the organisation also demonstrates her need to instinctively go along in any situation, rather than proactively question developments and posit alternatives. Change always involves a certain element of uncertainty; hence, it becomes important to (a) explore alternatives and think flexibly, and (b) take risks.

Since life itself is about growth and transformation, it would help to understand what stops us from embracing change. Is it self-doubt or the nagging need for a status quo? Or, is it the inability to manage intense emotions that arise during change? The good news is that, in all cases, there is a solution—if there is a will!

EMOTIONAL INTELLIGENCE AND CONFLICT

The Link between Emotional Intelligence and Conflict

The stories in this section depict two situations of conflict, which require skilled and balanced negotiation. In order to become a truly skilful negotiator in conflict situations, it is important not only to be able to use cognitive strategies, tools and techniques but also to be emotionally intelligent. The various skills, techniques and tools relating to becoming a more emotionally intelligent negotiator largely have to do with three broad areas of emotional intelligence: emotional awareness and objectivity, emotional management and empathy and self-expression to get through a difficult conversation.

Developing skills in negotiation can help you to resolve issues, bring about positive outcomes, attain the joys offered by relationships and spur the creativity that conflicts create. It may be helpful to observe yourself during the next conflicting situation you go through, decode the information about yourself that the situation provides and act to develop yourself. This could be the springboard to building relationships at the next level.

As you read the next few stories, try and identify the points at which the mastery or lack of emotional intelligence skills comes into play. How do these shape the outcome? What would you do in such a situation? What strategies would you employ to overcome the obstacles that arise?

Adam and Ramesh's Story: Win–Win

In the London office of a global IT company, with offices spread across the U.S., Europe and India, Adam's team had just landed a large-scale and complex project on customised database programming. To convince the client of their capability, Adam had even worked on building a test database. After six months of strenuous meetings and rigorous quality checks, the team made the final cut and got the contract. The project deadline was three months away. They got to work instantly and began to put the database in place, ensuring that it was source-controlled.

The weeks flew by as they worked day and night to complete the gargantuan task. After the development stage, they quality-checked the product to ensure there were no bugs or regressions. Unfortunately, they found an error. Adam advised the team to find the source of the problem immediately, which, after much deliberation, was narrowed down to the tool they had used. This new tool had only recently been released in the market. The team had decided to use it so as to ensure they would deliver the best and latest to their valued customer. However, neither Adam nor his team members were completely familiar with the tool's interface. Adam asked the team to learn more about the tool and its inner workings. At the end of a tension-filled week, Wilson, a member of Adam's team, came to Adam's office. He explained that the problem in the tool had been identified and could be fixed. Unfortunately, it meant that the team would have to start all over again, right from the beginning. Hence, the project would take an additional two months to complete, while the deadline loomed just three weeks ahead of them. Adam felt this was unacceptable and pushed his team to complete the project by the original deadline.

A few days before the deadline, the customer called Adam to check on the project's progress. Adam falsely convinced himself and the client that the project would be completed in time. Pleased, the client informed Adam that he would come to their office to see the final database on the project completion date. Adam confronted his team for a status update; the team told him that despite their best efforts, the project would still take another month to complete. Beside himself with worry, Adam stayed up the next few nights thinking about his options. Finally, on the morning of D-Day, he feigned an emergency and cancelled the meeting with the client.

Matters had finally come to a head: the project was far from complete and the client was expecting results any day. Seeing no recourse, Adam went to his manager and apprised him of the whole sorry situation. The manager was furious. In all their interactions, Adam had always maintained that the project was on track. He had not kept internal or external stakeholders in the loop. If the problem had been identified a month ago, why was he only hearing of it now? Adam was immediately taken off the project.

In this scenario, marked by mounting tensions, a demotivated and overworked team and a customer waiting to hear bad news, Ramesh was called in as the new account manager. The task assigned to him was a tough one: remedy the situation, pacify the client and ensure that company losses are minimised.

Ramesh related the rest of the story to us six months after the fact. As you read on, pay special note to Ramesh's remarks (italicised below), which clearly outline his analysis, approach and thought process towards solving these various problems.

While the company was prepared to lose money on this project, Ramesh set his goals for this account—fulfil the three main criteria, but also make as much profit for the company as was initially envisaged. He reflected that not carrying past baggage was an advantage. At the same time, not having an existing relationship with the client could be a disadvantage as he did not possess the levers to understand the client.

Ramesh's remarks: Being emotionally attached to our solution/ideas can be a dangerous trap. It creates an internal conflict between defending our own stance as an expert and truly listening to the issues at hand and working at a win–win solution.

In this situation, trust had been seriously damaged. Ramesh knew his first job was to rebuild this trust deficit. He realised that by not getting the delivery on time, the client would not only miss an internal deadline but also cut a sorry figure before his own seniors and his colleagues.

Ramesh's remarks: Often, we focus on the tangible part of the problem and not enough on what this means to the client.

While listening with empathy and expressing regret was obviously critical, what made the client really open up was the fact that Ramesh expressed genuine regret at the impact of this delay on the client and asked whether he and his team could do anything to help the client internally. The process of creating a turnaround in the client's feelings naturally involved a number of conversations.

Ramesh's remarks: How often, in such situations, we avoid such meetings, assuming that we need to give the client some time and space. And how tough we find it to be the object of the client's ire. Emotions take time to settle down, and our ability to manage our own emotions and enable the client to manage his can reduce the time it takes to achieve the turnaround.

What really helped the client move into a more logical conversation was that Ramesh shared the details of the problem with him and offered him choices. Ramesh repeated the following statement in a number of different ways. 'You were so excited about this project—I know this is tough for you. What opportunities can we create that will help you with this?' In the following discussions, Ramesh also shared his own views with the client so that they could start working on a solution together.

Ramesh's remarks: We were in a trench, and he was out of it. We needed to involve him so we could both then plan how to get out—together. This involved helping him understand 'how' we got into it and 'why' this will not happen again.

Steering the conversation towards 'choice' is key. How can we give you a beautiful pot instead of the urn that you previously wanted? When the client sees choices, it helps to pull them into solution mode. Then, both parties can look at overcoming the problem together. Co-creating the solution with the client is really the point at which re-establishment of trust begins.

Ramesh's next step was to ensure that the project was made profitable, while aligning with the client's new needs at the same time. Meeting the objectives for the client as well as for the company was critical.

Ramesh's remarks: Real win–win happens when you can confidently state your terms, not assuming that the client cannot give a better price—especially if you have offered genuine value. Quite often, in such situations, we fall into a self-created trap where pleasing the client means placing ourselves in a difficult spot. That can only be a temporary win—as a win–lose eventually moves towards a lose–lose situation in the long run.

At this point, simple arithmetic helped Ramesh and the team to identify the inefficiencies that are inherent in any process and can be leveraged for profitability. On the one hand, monetising productivity helped in working at profitability. On the other hand, selling the benefits of the proposal to the internal team brought in huge commitment. This was Ramesh's solution in order to meet his personal goal of completing a 'profitable project'.

A few months later and at a higher price, the project was completed—profitably, as Ramesh had envisioned and expected. The client was happy, and the chief technology officer (CTO) of the client company launched the database for the entire company. During the launch, the client mentioned that 'this was a great solution created in the shortest possible time.' Ramesh, of course, was absolutely delighted.

Behind the Scenes

This real-life story was told to us by Ramesh. First and foremost, his awareness of his own emotions helped him considerably to abstain from becoming defensive. Besides emotional awareness, Ramesh's problem-solving skills were enhanced by his high objectivity. Not being led emotionally allowed him to work dispassionately with the issues at hand, creating a solution that was acceptable to him and his customer. He worked *with* his client to co-create effective resolutions to the problem.

Ramesh's objectivity saved him from falling into a common trap and thinking, 'I can never make mistakes. I am the expert and I should know all.' Very often 'experts' assume they should know all the answers; they are not allowed to err. This assumption stems from low objectivity, and leaders often ignore the assumptions that their decisions were based on.

Ramesh's high levels of self-expression and self-appraisal allowed him to state his terms to the customer and ask for the deserved price, based on the belief that he was delivering genuine value. At the same time, Ramesh was able to empathise with the client. He let the client vent his feelings and understood that this meant a lot to the client. Once his feelings were out in the open and acknowledged, the client was able to move on. The balance between allowing the client to vent and giving him choices to move on is a fine one—and often difficult to achieve. Patience and deep listening give us cues about when and how to move on.

Let us look at another example of emotional intelligence in action in a negotiation.

Anmol's Story: Captain Cool

It all began with that one phone call where Nikhil, the client, called up Anmol and said, 'Let's call it off!' The entire team was anxious as they overhead Anmol talking to Nikhil. Their well-laid plans of achieving the quarterly target were suddenly thrown into disarray.

Anmol's heart sank as Nikhil said those words. If they did not get this account, it was the end of the world. The stakes were simply too high. Anmol and his team had given it their all in the last four months. Nikhil was exerting immense pressure, and Anmol and the organisation were on the back foot. They had already invested a lot into getting this account, in terms of time, money and energy.

Nikhil had always dealt in extremes. To add to that, he was emotionally volatile. He was supposed to email the contract that day after a discussion on minor variables. Surely, he could not be calling it off at this stage! Previously, Anmol had been unaccustomed to paying attention to his internal state, but he now realised how angry he was—almost ready to explode. He wanted to shout at, insult and intimidate Nikhil on the phone.

However, Anmol realised that he had to deal with this differently. This account was too important, and the situation needed to be handled delicately. He could not let his anger or ego act against his own best interests. Somehow, he needed to keep his cool.

Anmol took a deep breath and quickly assessed his predicament, looking for a solution. He could not entirely curb his anxiety, but he paid attention to and understood the uncomfortable thoughts that were creeping into his mind.

Then, he replied, 'Nikhil, it must be hard for you to say this after four months of interaction. Let's do some creative problem-solving so that we can both benefit. You know this contract is equally important for both of us. I know you have only recently joined the organisation and this could mean a lot to you. From my end, you know I cannot come down further on the price and threatening me would not help. Let's solve this together—please?'

There was a long pause, during which Anmol held his breath. Then, Nikhil said, 'All right, let's figure this out together.' Anmol exhaled quietly and resumed the conversation. The two of them spoke for a long time. Anmol tried to understand Nikhil's point of view and gave him a patient hearing. At the same time, he also handled all the pressure tactics that Nikhil repeatedly tried to use on him. After an intense discussion, Anmol and Nikhil were able to arrive at a solution that was perceived to be a win–win for both parties.

Behind the Scenes

In the above story, through his firm and empathetic reply, Anmol got Nikhil's attention. Pushing back actually helped the situation. It made Nikhil realise that he too needed the collaboration to work, and the suggestion of win–win was appealing. Anmol's ability to express his emotions and thoughts and defend his views assertively was the game changer. At the same time, Anmol also empathised with Nikhil, understanding that he had recently joined the organisation and this could mean a lot to him.

Know More: The 50-50 of Negotiation

In his book *The Highwaymen*, which profiles leading players in the field of communications and information technology, Ken Auletta quotes the investment banker Felix Rohatyn (who, while the book was being written, was involved in the attempted takeover of Paramount Communications by Viacom International) as follows: 'Most deals are fifty percent emotion and fifty percent economics.' Rohatyn was talking about the personalities involved and about the shifting dynamics of the protracted negotiations that were being conducted for the highest possible stakes.

EMOTIONAL INTELLIGENCE AND CUSTOMER SERVICE

The Link between Emotional Intelligence and Customer Service

The stories in this section present examples of customer service driven by emotional intelligence. All service organisations agree that each individual contributes to the success of an organisation. The belief, in the individual, that 'I make a difference' combined with the feeling of caring for another person can drive great customer service behaviours.

The emotional intelligence competencies that enable the right behaviours in situations of customer service are empathy, emotional self-awareness, impulse control and optimism. Leaders strong in these areas often take up caring professions where 'servicing society' motivates them to attain great heights.

These competencies may be challenging for people to develop if their entire interpersonal competencies are low. For a person to provide good customer service, it is integral for him/her to possess a liking for people and the ability to see interconnectedness in life. The natural desire to help others flows from these qualities. Perhaps that is the biggest reason why the service industry in particular bases hiring on intrinsic qualities such as positive outlook, people concern, problem-solving and confidence. Service competencies are difficult to build if there is no inherent orientation supporting their development.

As you read the next few stories, try and identify the points at which the mastery or lack of emotional intelligence skills comes into play. How do these shape the outcome? What would you do in such a situation? What strategies would you employ to overcome the obstacles that arise?

Kamala's Story: Hidden Hero

I had been in the emergency wing at the hospital for hours, waiting to hear about a relative who was undergoing surgery. I desperately needed to visit the ladies' washroom—something I had been putting off for hours. The nightmarish experience of visiting toilets in public places is not new to most Indians. Many of us screw up our noses at the disgusting sights and smells that greet us whenever we attempt to respond to the call of nature in a public washroom.

After having postponed the visit as long as was humanly possible, I decided I simply had to go to the washroom. I must not forget to mention that while pacing the visitors' corridor for a long time, I had been counting the comings and goings of the women visiting the washroom. I counted at least 15 visitors every four minutes. 'How come there is no hospital attendant who has gone in even once in the three hours that I have been here,' I wondered.

After having visualised what I expected to encounter—leaky taps, wet floors, unbearable stench and muck-filled pots—I steeled myself to enter this grand site. As I opened the door apprehensively, my first surprise was seeing the washroom attendant (I later found out her name was Kamala), sitting on a low stool. She immediately rose to greet me with a pleasant 'Good afternoon, ma'am'.

'Oh, good afternoon,' I replied.
'How is your patient?' she asked.
A bit surprised by her concern, I responded, 'Fine, thank you.'
'One minute, ma'am, let me sanitise this for you,' Kamala said.

Promptly going into one of the toilet stalls, she sprayed some disinfectant on the seat, wiped it clean, smiled again and exited. I looked around disbelievingly—an absolutely dry, clean and fresh-smelling toilet! My surprise did not end there—a drip-free tap, soap and tissues to clean my hands awaited me to complete an experience that made me feel pleasantly surprised and very relieved.

'Thank you—I really appreciate how clean you keep this washroom as well as your prompt and willing service. Who has trained you so well? Is it the hospital or your own upbringing that makes you so devoted to your work?' I asked Kamala.

'Ma'am, I have worked in a few hospitals before this,' Kamala explained. 'My son was also very unwell a few years back. When I took him to the two hospitals that I had worked in, I was treated really badly. No one understood my anguish, and the hospital staff would shout at me constantly. Later, my son got well and I joined this hospital. I vowed to myself that I am going to make every visitor here feel good. From personal experience, I know that people in a hospital go through anxiety, anguish, suffering and pain. The least I can do is to reach out to them, through my work. Their acknowledgement and appreciation will always help me and my son—this I know. That is why I choose to do my best in my work and do so happily.'

For a few moments, I simply looked at this amazing, inspiring woman in silent admiration. Then, I held out my hand to clasp Kamala's, murmured a prayer of gratitude and thanked her profusely.

Behind the Scenes

Who says that leadership behaviours reside only at the top echelons of the organisation? Day after day, stories enacted by human beings at all levels, and sometimes at the front-line levels of organisations, have a distinct and deep impact.

Kamala's story touched me deeply. Immediately, I felt like emulating her and harnessing the positivity of her thoughts in my own life. How illuminating, touching and exciting to see a 'larger' purpose in contexts that many of us consider so 'small'. How powerful were Kamala's honest expression, genuine emotional sharing and dedication and joy in the work she did! Her leadership behaviour continues to inspire me to this day.

Ganesh's Story: The Extra Mile

Set in one of the five-star deluxe and luxury hotel chains of India, this tale is about a gentleman called Ganesh. Ganesh had been working with the hotel for 15 years. He had started out as an apprentice and was now an assistant, working in the laundry department of housekeeping. He always had a smile for the guests and for his colleagues.

One day, while working on the ironing machine, he noticed that a button was missing from the jacket he was ironing for the guest. He immediately highlighted this to the supervisor. The supervisor recommended that Ganesh inform the guest.

Ganesh called the guest and told him about the missing button. The guest became very worried because he had to wear the jacket for a function in the evening. The laundry department did not have any buttons that matched the design on the jacket.

After getting off his shift at 4 p.m., Ganesh went to a market near the hotel and bought a button that was similar (but not identical) to the other buttons on the jacket. He went back to the hotel, changed into his uniform again and went up to the guest's room. He showed the button to the guest and asked if he would want this stitched on as a replacement. The guest was fine with the design, but he wanted all the buttons changed so they would be identical. 'Certainly, sir,' said Ganesh immediately and went away.

He walked back to the market to buy the requisite number of buttons. After coming back to the hotel, he stitched on all the buttons and had the jacket ready for the guest by 8 p.m.— well in time for the guest's evening engagement. Needless to say, the guest was delighted with this experience.

What Ganesh did not know was that this guest was a mystery auditor who was doing a global audit for the hotel chain. When the auditor filed his report, he gave the hotel a glowing review and Ganesh was rated as the Best Employee. He had brought laurels to his department and to the hotel. During the felicitation, the general manager asked, 'Ganesh, what prompted you to go out of your way and beyond your call of duty?'

'Our job is to ensure that every guest is delighted, and if I have an opportunity to do this, I am only doing my job,' Ganesh replied. The auditor testified that what differentiated Ganesh's action was the fact that his passion and the desire to create guest delight truly came from his heart.

Behind the Scenes

What makes Ganesh go beyond the call of duty and reach out to people with a desire to help, while so many others only focus energies on themselves and can easily tire if asked to extend themselves in relationships at home or at work? The answer may be a combination of various factors—but the key skill needed in these situations is undoubtedly empathy. A natural inclination towards compassion and caring along with a need to help others and make a difference to them and to society drives genuinely excellent customer service. These characteristics define both Ganesh and Kamala (from the previous story).

Know More: Empathy and Compassion Enough for Millions

Mother Teresa knew at the age of 12 that her calling was to be a missionary to spread the love of Christ. To this end, she left her hometown at the age of 18 and joined the Sisters of Loreto, an Irish community of nuns with missions in India. The suffering and poverty she witnessed in Calcutta made such a deep impression on her that in 1948 she devoted herself to working amongst the poorest of the poor in the slums of Calcutta. Soon, she was joined by voluntary helpers, and financial support was also forthcoming. This made it possible for her to extend the scope of her work and reach such great heights. Mother Teresa's empathy and compassion enabled her to spend her entire life working with those on the lowest rungs of the socio-economic ladder and benefit society at large.

EMOTIONAL INTELLIGENCE AND PRODUCTIVITY

The Link between Emotional Intelligence and Productivity

The story in this section illustrates how emotional intelligence is linked with productivity. The emotional intelligence competencies that come into play are achievement drive, optimism and self-appraisal.

As consultants working in the field of emotional intelligence, we are often surprised by the low 'achievement drive' scores we find through our individual EQ assessment tool. Individuals with lower scores in this component often feel they may be drifting, believing that they are not driving their own lives. Conversely, studies reveal that star performers at all levels are found to possess higher EQ scores, and that of all the competencies required for high performance, 67 per cent are those to do with EQ.[1]

Do people know what truly drives them, what they want their lives to be like in the long term? Is it easy for them to create linkages between their strengths and their dreams so as to push their energies towards their own goals? Quite often, amongst the individuals we have worked with, the answer has been 'no'. When we have probed further, we have found that the goals individuals often chase are determined by their society, bosses and parents, and in most cases, people have not even asked themselves the question: 'What do I really want?' In Pratiek's story below, we will take a look at the importance of having a clear answer to these questions, and how this clarity is integral in shaping and directing your professional life.

As you read, try and identify the points at which the mastery or lack of emotional intelligence skills shapes the story. What would you do in such a situation? What strategies would you employ to overcome the obstacles that come up?

Pratiek's Story: Staying True to What Excites You

Pratiek was a high-achieving manager of a critical vertical in a global knowledge process outsourcing (KPO). He had proven himself in that role by meeting goals related to turn around time (TAT) and client satisfaction quarter on quarter for eight quarters. He had been instrumental in building his

---

[1] Daniel Jay Goleman, 1995, *Emotional Intelligence: Why It Can Matter More Than IQ*, London: Bloomsbury Publishing India Private Limited.

team from 20 to 60 people in just two years, to meet the growing client requirements. His team held him in utmost regard and were inspired and engaged despite the fact that he was a hard taskmaster, demanding very high quality levels. The team had grown well under his demanding style.

His growth and success in a crucial role prompted the organisation to put him on the fast track for development and move him into another very critical role from the organisational standpoint. The new role required him to consolidate work being done by various verticals so that the organisation got better leverage out of the system and could provide higher value services to the clients. The role required a high level of strategic thinking, knowledge management, interaction with clients and working with internal stakeholders at the peer level.

The move was seen as a coveted one, since it provided a line of sight to the firm's entire value chain and an opportunity to create significant changes in the way services were being provided to customers. Pratiek, however, felt a sense of trepidation taking it on. His manager and the larger leadership team spent considerable time with him highlighting the significance of the role to the firm's long-term strategy.

Ostensibly, it was a great playing field for a performer of Pratiek's calibre and potential—something that should have motivated him to create success from the word go. In the first quarter, Pratiek lived up to expectations—he made great inroads into hitherto unchartered territory. He created an extensive blueprint for the way forward on the consolidation of all verticals to enhance the value of services for customers.

However, by the second and then the third quarter, things started to go amiss; he did not feel the same sense of excitement and energy while attempting to bring the blueprint to life. He felt the need to constantly charge himself and also to seek out his manager more and more for guidance and feedback.

In fact, by the end of the third quarter, Pratiek was certain he needed to take remedial action before everything went awry and out of control. It was at that time that he took an

EQ assessment tool and got into an executive coaching engagement. Very soon into the feedback and coaching process, it became evident that Pratiek's goal and the role did not excite him. While he understood the value of this role for the company, it was not a goal that he was passionate about and hence he could not sustain his level of commitment and energy. His high performance in the first few months was largely due to his sense of alignment to the organisation.

Since Pratiek was high on self-awareness, he quickly recognised that he must take action to address the problem. High self-appraisal also made it easy for him to seek out his manager for feedback and also agree for a coaching engagement to help him through his predicament. He did not feel threatened with either the feedback or the fact that he was getting into a development process despite being a high-potential team member.

He realised, through his reflections during the coaching engagement, that goals that were quantifiable—that is, sales-related goals, client satisfaction leading to repeat business, building a team to meet increased client requirements—excited him the most. He felt he could completely own these goals and had, in the past, done exceedingly well in making them a reality.

In fact, so high was Pratiek's drive for these goals that he even managed to work around his relatively low interpersonal skills. Hence, he was able to lead his team to challenging targets. However, in this new role, his low drive for the goal could not be mitigated by his ability to set clear targets, plan, review and problem-solve (all of these skills he possessed and had brought to bear in his earlier roles).

Pratiek was fortunate to have a highly supportive manager who thought it prudent to deploy Pratiek's talents, abilities and skills where they would consistently create value for the firm and for him. The management team decided to create a career path for him that would help him leverage his abilities towards the firm's growth. They then focused on identifying another high-potential manager who would be more aligned to the role that Pratiek had been earlier offered.

It was only a matter of time before Pratiek rose to a leadership level, and today, he continues to drive the firm's growth by performing roles that drive him and enable him to create high performance and productivity for himself and the firm.

Behind the Scenes

As seen in Pratiek's story, individual attempts to enhance performance and productivity often fall short as they tend to miss the major driver for achievement and therefore productivity. Put simply, this driver is the need to achieve, and the ownership of goals.

So, whereas having clearly defined goals, goal alignment with stakeholders, planning for goals and reviewing progress are all *prerequisites* for an individual or an organisation to enhance productivity, these are not *sufficient drivers* for high performance and productivity.

The crucial missing links lie in the following:

- A person completely wanting to achieve the goal and owning the goal.
- A person setting goals that they can influence with their ability. This determined, results-driven approach is almost invariably present in the character make-up of all successful business people and entrepreneurs.
- A person asking for and receiving continuous and constructive feedback. Feedback is essential, because it enables the measurement of success. Achievement-motivated people constantly seek improvements and ways of doing things better.
- A person who has the ability to be in a good mood and in general optimistic through setbacks that they may encounter in pursuit of their goal.

In a nutshell, individuals such as Pratiek, who possess a high-achievement drive and self-awareness will take complete responsibility of their goals, make things happen and get results. This extends to getting results through the organisation of other people and resources. Therefore, the link between emotional intelligence and productivity cannot be stressed enough.

EMOTIONAL INTELLIGENCE AND PERFORMANCE MANAGEMENT

The Link between Emotional Intelligence and Performance Management

The story in this section demonstrates how emotional intelligence corresponds to performance conversations. The emotional intelligence competencies that come into play are self-expression, objectivity, empathy, optimism and achievement drive, which are key components for good performance conversations.

Our experience of working with organisations over the years has revealed big gaps in leaders' abilities to manage performance and productivity. In this next story, we meet Anu, a manager at a media organisation, who conducts a difficult conversation with one of her long-time employees about his performance. Through this story, we will explore some of the reasons performance conversations can be so difficult to handle effectively, and how important it is as a manager to be able to do so.

As you read, try and identify the points at which the mastery or lack of emotional intelligence skills shapes the story. What would you do in such a situation? What strategies would you employ to overcome the obstacles that come up?

Anu's Story: The Truth Hurts But Also Heals

As Anu walked into the office that morning, she knew that it was *the* day. Anu had always been a straightforward person, known for calling a spade a spade. There was a key decision to be made today regarding two of her team members—Rajat and Chetan—and the outcome was clear in her mind.

Rajat and Chetan had both joined *Nominist* magazine in July 2007 as management trainees and had become fast friends from the beginning.

As trainees, they each had their unique strengths. Rajat was a conscientious worker. He paid great attention to details, even if it meant putting in late hours. He was known for his slow turnaround time, but in a small organisation such as *Nominist*, the superior quality of his work did not go unnoticed.

Chetan, however, was a smart and overconfident worker who believed himself to be on the fast track to success. He would take time out to have conversations with his seniors and also to network and get his work done through other people.

At first, people were amazed at how efficient Chetan was compared to Rajat. But slowly, Chetan's peers began to dislike his delegation and pushing back style. His seniors too realised that his knowledge of any subject was superficial at best as he avoided any hands-on work. However, despite feedback from his managers and peers, Chetan felt that Rajat's way of functioning was archaic. Meanwhile, Rajat emerged as a dependable and trustworthy resource. As the days went by, Rajat began to receive the kind of positive attention that Chetan could not catch.

Used to being in the limelight, Chetan began to feel ignored. By their second year at *Nominist*, Rajat and Chetan's friendship was a thing of the past—replaced by competition and envy on Chetan's part. Envy turned to rage for Chetan when, in July 2009, Rajat was chosen for the position of Assistant Manager—Operations over him. Chetan was outraged—he had never seen Rajat as an exceptional asset to the company and hence felt that the company was deliberately trying to crush his brilliance. Although Chetan too was promoted six months later, he never got over the humiliation of being chosen last.

Cut to July 2011. Two years after the last promotion, it was time for the move to the next level, Manager—Operations, and it was up to Anu to make a recommendation to the general manager. Because Anu had been managing the duo for two years now, she was familiar with the strengths and weaknesses of both.

During this period, Rajat had been working quietly and steadily. His key quality was that he was willing to work hard—on the tasks that were given to him, as well as on the feedback. Being open to others' advice had helped him grow and overcome his limitations. He had been able to *develop* certain leadership qualities that he did not naturally possess—for example, being able to effectively communicate the advantages of his proposals to key stakeholders.

Chetan, however, had grown little from the time he had joined *Nominist*. While he achieved most of his results in the beginning of his career, he was defensive, and at times even aggressive, in the face of feedback. His last promotion had been based on his tenure in the company, rather than on his performance.

Chetan had made no secret of his disappointment the last time round, and everyone knew that he expected to be chosen first this time. This promotion would mean that he would be Rajat's boss for at least a year before the next performance evaluation, something that Chetan felt was important to restore his position in the organisation.

Of course, what he did not know was that Anu had decided to recommend Rajat.

So on the big day, Anu walked into her office and wrote the recommendation mail to the general manager. As she clicked on 'send', she felt that it would be unfair for Chetan to hear of this through the grapevine. She thought of what she wanted to convey to Chetan. It was true she was irritated by his behaviour, but she could see that he had potential that could be harnessed if he was willing.

She picked up the phone and called him to her office. Chetan strode in confidently, expecting to hear 'congratulations'. As Anu broke the news to Chetan, his face fell. He was totally shocked and outraged. Anu realised that he needed time to absorb the news. She calmly allowed him to speak non-stop for the next 10 minutes about how unfair the company had been on repeated occasions. He had given four years of his professional life to *Nominist* and they had never returned the favour. He could not stand this any longer and threatened to leave. 'What else do you expect me to do?' he asked.

Anu could feel her temper rising but resisted the urge to lash back at him. She paused a minute and took a deep breath. She had initially wanted to explain why she had made that decision. However, she could see that Chetan was not in a state to listen. She patiently heard everything he had to say and then asked to speak her piece. Since Chetan had expressed himself already, he agreed that there was nothing for him to do but listen.

Anu explained that she saw Chetan as an intelligent person who did not use his gifts. She empathised with his disappointment over the 2009 promotion. However, she observed that he had shunned the feedback he had received in the past few years and not made any effort to improve his performance. By not getting into the details and depths of various proposals, he appeared indifferent to taking complete responsibility. Anu listed the qualities that made one a good candidate for leadership positions; learning from feedback and striving to improve was one of them. Chetan was expected to take feedback in his stride and work on doing things differently. She asked, 'Do you feel like you are giving it your all?'

Anu laid out her cards on the table—If Chetan was willing to change and work hard, she would help him work on his strengths and actively coach him on his areas of development. With some efforts, she was certain Chetan could become a high-performing member of the organisation. Otherwise, he was free to make his way outside *Nominist*, if he so desired.

She then stepped out to get a cup of coffee, giving him five minutes alone to think about what he wanted to do.

Chetan was taken aback by her straightforward manner. He was not sure how to react. On the one hand, he was offended by how the company was treating him, but on the other, he somehow trusted Anu—his internal feelings were telling him that there was some truth in Anu's feedback. He knew that Anu was a great coach—he had seen Rajat flourish under her guidance.

When Anu walked back in, Chetan told her that he had decided to make an honest effort to improve. They sat down together to chalk out a plan for the road ahead.

Behind the Scenes

Anu's story highlights how important it is for managers to have effective and clear conversations with their employees. A common roadblock that managers face with respect to performance conversations is the inability to give clear, direct and effective feedback. Culturally, talking straight is not looked upon as being polite, deferential or even considerate. Perhaps this belief could be translating into performance conversations being long-winded, not to the point and often confusing for the individual receiving the feedback. In our many years of working with Indian organisations, we have found a common weak spot in how Indian leaders manage performance and productivity. Two common causes for this weakness are given below:

- One of the consequences of the Indian growth story is that it catapulted people into leadership roles that they were not necessarily equipped to handle. As pressures of performance grew, the activity trap ensured that focus on the 'important' gave way to focus on the 'urgent'. As a result, this change of focus distanced both productivity and performance in the bargain.
- The lack of focus on coaching and developing others has lead to sub-optimum levels of competence, high complacency and low accountability.

The leadership challenge of focusing on the right issues, while developing people to enable them to take on more responsibilities and achieve higher results efficiently, continues to exist. Mature leaders, who are not fraught with the fear of losing their jobs in an extremely competitive environment, are seen to develop their teams. Courageous and empathic leaders, who speak their mind while exploring the feelings and views of their subordinates effectively, develop their people. Optimistic leaders, who see things objectively, yet push the bar for their teams believing in their capabilities, develop their people. But most of all, leaders who enjoy people and the process of giving of themselves to see others grow develop others. Such leaders have to be strong in emotional intelligence, as a number of components such as objectivity, self-expression, achievement drive, optimism, empathy and interpersonal skills are required to be a truly successful leader.

EMOTIONAL INTELLIGENCE AND INSPIRATION

The Link between Emotional Intelligence and Inspiration

The story in this section illustrates the importance of a leader's role in igniting passion within the organisation and ensuring that dynamic emotions are directed towards shared goals to create results. In this case, the emotional intelligence competencies that come into play are optimism, achievement drive, empathy, self-expression and self-reliance.

The question is *Who inspires?* In this next story, we explore the answer to this essential question.

As you read, try and identify the points at which the mastery or lack of emotional intelligence skills shapes the story. What would you do in such a situation? What strategies would you employ to overcome the obstacles that come up?

One CEO's Story: Getting to the Heart of Inspiration

An EQ assessment discussion involving the CEO of a telecom company in India brought some interesting insights to light. The CEO had scored high in empathy—a score of 9.5 out of 10, with 10 being the highest.

Reflecting on his score, he deliberated, 'Actually, I can really relate to this, and also cannot stress enough the role of empathy in inspiring teams to achieve seemingly unachievable goals.'

After some more prodding, he related the following story: 'Only last year, I found myself in a tough situation. I had to convince my head of departments (HODs) to take on higher targets than the previous year, a year in which we had done phenomenally well. This was the result of a recent board meeting in which the directors and shareholders had given the diktat that we could not afford to let the momentum slow down. The previous year's results were stupendous and our organisation had the first-mover advantage. However, this year, the big players had plans of hitting the market with strong marketing and price-cut strategies. I was not sure how we were going to manage this goal—but hope and optimism have always served me well. I became aware of a surge of adrenaline that ran through me, building excitement towards meeting the challenge.

'I decided to call for a daylong retreat with the team to congratulate them on the previous year's performance and to set targets for the coming year. I must confess, I was apprehensive as I knew that corridor talks were getting louder. Everyone was worried about how difficult it would be to beat larger companies' competitive strategies, not to mention their salaries. There were fears that our company results were bound to be impacted in a big way. I began by communicating the delight of the board members and their congratulations on a great job, achieved through the passion and hard work of the entire team and organisation. I also communicated that there existed a great opportunity in the market and having started well, we were perfectly poised to go for the bigger market shares and higher results. I declared that we would project a growth of 20 per cent from the previous year—something that with our experience and teamwork should be possible.

'I was prepared for resistance, but had possibly underestimated the extent of objections that I was to face. I could read a blank "no" on everyone's faces. I made a quick assessment of the situation and realised that I had to quickly change tracks or risk speaking only to myself. I knew that no one would buy into whatever else I had to say unless I completely understood the perspective of each HOD present.

'I took a deep breath and closed the door. After a pause, I immediately summarised my observations of the group's feelings, and noticed a few of them nod vigorously. Most of them looked visibly relieved that I realised how tough their situation was. I then told them that we would not proceed until each one of them had had a chance to voice their views and concerns. We spent the next four hours carefully listening to each other and understanding the concerns. I could see their point of view as I too knew that the new strategy was risky. I summarised my understanding of their fears, ensuring that each one of them felt *understood*.

'I have often experienced in situations of conflict, that when people feel understood, their responsiveness, openness and ability to listen to the other points of view greatly improves. Slowly, I could see that in our discussions, questions were shifting from self and individual views to common goals.

'I knew that now was the time to shift gears. Taking charge, I explained the rationale behind the new strategy, enumerating the big goal that we must achieve. Shifting gears also meant that I had to make an internal shift and truly believe that we can achieve our "audacious" goal; my tone had to communicate this conviction. Creating a vision of the goal, I built excitement by carefully stating how and why this could be possible. Passionately, I projected full confidence in the team's abilities and the advantages that we, as a company, had.

'I then asked the group to spend the next hour deliberating on the goal—if we have to achieve our goals, what is it that we needed from the organisation, but more critically from ourselves?

'The next hour and a half was simply amazing. The group worked hard at solving problems around all perceived obstacles. I continued to build confidence in the team's abilities to grow the business, and together we created inspiration and excitement to move ahead towards the next phase.

'What do you think happened that year? Well, we did not achieve the 20 per cent growth that we were aiming for—but the upside is that we were not far behind. We established ourselves in a growing, highly competitive market, using our strengths and experience—but, most importantly, our passion to win.'

Behind the Scenes

As seen in this story, the answer to *Who inspires?* is simple. Most certainly, it is a person who feels inspired himself. So, necessarily, this is a person who has high self-belief, communicates positive energy and hope and can envision a lofty goal that pulls everyone together through the power of achieving something 'big'. Such a visionary leader dares, he shares positive emotions and, even more importantly, he builds *trust*. Through an impeccable alignment of thoughts, feelings and words, such a leader creates a belief in others that they can achieve the impossible—leading to their *wanting* to achieve this as well.

The ability to experience intense positive feelings that energise the self and others, as well as the courage to dare to have big goals, defines the inspirational leader. Such a leader is aware of his emotions, can build on positive emotions and can communicate and create positive feelings in others. This does not mean that such a leader needs to thump the table or raise his voice for effect, but it certainly means that regardless of anything, the leader demonstrates strong belief in what he is propagating because he has true conviction in his vision. Thus, the strong linkage between inspiration and emotions is definite.

Conclusion

As we come to the end of the book, we ask ourselves the same question that prompted us to write the book in the first place—Has emotional intelligence received its due? In our opinion, the answer is a definite *no*. While emotional intelligence has been studied by various fields—including philosophy, religion, psychology and business—it has not achieved its right place or importance in the real world, perhaps for the following reasons:

1. This is seen as an intangible concept, and in this fast-paced world when everyone is scurrying around to make things work—it is so much more exciting to deal with the here and now, immediate and seemingly unavoidable urgency we create around ourselves.

2. The process of confronting ourselves is never easy, and changing ourselves even more arduous. Who *really* wants to know what I could have done better in any situation? There seems to be some relief in blaming others, not taking responsibilities and thinking—*if only...*

3. Emotions are scary. They seem to overtake us, overwhelm us and drive our behaviours in a way that is not in our control. Therefore, isn't it easier then to dismiss them?

So even though every discipline talks about the relevance, importance and the advantage of emotional intelligence, in the real world, the game that is played is *Prove it if you can*.

While the above could be debatable to a few, no one can deny that in families, societies and organisations—emotions have either created huge value or wreaked havoc. Most of us would have witnessed cases of siblings bringing down families because of lack of emotional resilience, or accounts of leaders destroying value in societies, corporations and countries.

We also know of leaders who, by their ability to demonstrate passion, caring, compassion, inspiration and, also at times, through appropriate use of fear and anger, drive people, organisations and societies to unbelievable heights. History is replete with accounts of leaders who have used both their heads and their hearts to manage complexities and lead people courageously to unchartered courses.

This book was not been created to prove *why* emotional intelligence is important for oneself and at the workplace. Our experiences with the relatively fewer leaders, who consciously work on themselves and in this area, give us more than enough evidence to say it works. We only hope that through the stories of others, you would also be able to craft your own stories—be the person you wish to be, in the way you wish to be, to achieve the goals you wish to achieve.

Authenticity, awareness and sensitivity are the attributes that emotional intelligence can help us build towards our journey to success. Consciously working on this, especially at our workplace, can help us build a culture and engagement that nothing else can. Bringing out our *humane* side is the best way of being human. We hope that some of these stories have also brought out these elements for you.

Finally, emotional intelligence requires courage, and you will go only as deep as you dare. Hopefully, the storytelling style inspired you to reflect and encouraged you to change.

Hopefully, you enjoyed the book!

About the Author

Neeta **Mohla** has worked extensively in the area of people and leadership development, interpersonal dynamics, coaching and counselling. She works with individuals, teams and organisations, enabling them to enhance capabilities through a much better understanding of themselves and others.

In 2000, Neeta established TMI in India. Recognising her entrepreneurial contributions, Bharat Nirman awarded her the 'Women Entrepreneur of the Year'. Over the past 30 years, Neeta has led several research projects on leadership behaviours of Indian leaders and emotional intelligence in the Indian context, and has published papers for the Forum of Emotional Intelligence Learning (FEIL). She has delivered over 200 programmes on emotional intelligence in India and abroad, beneficial for leaders from different spheres—corporate, public, academic, among others. Besides her significant contributions on emotional intelligence, Neeta also has experience in counselling people through her association with Sanjivini, a non-government organisation helping people in emotional distress. She is a certified emotional intelligence coach and facilitator.